# EMERGENCIES

by Linda Peterson

Series developed by Peggy Schmidt

**Peterson's**

Princeton, New Jersey

A New Century Communications Book

# Other titles in
# this series include:

## CARS
## COMPUTERS
## FASHION
## FITNESS
## HEALTH CARE
## KIDS
## MUSIC

Peterson, Linda, 1949–
    Emergencies / by Linda Peterson.
        p.    cm.—(Careers without college)
    ISBN 1-56079-252-3 (pbk.) : $7.95
    1. Assistance in emergencies—Vocational guidance—United States. 2. Police—Vocational guidance—United States. 3. Fire extinction—Vocational guidance—United States. 4. Emergency medical services—Vocational guidance—United States. I. Title. II. Series.
HV551.3.P47   1993
363.2'4—dc20                     93-7077
                                      CIP

Art direction: Linda Huber
Cover photo: Bryce Flynn Photography
Cover and interior design: Greg Wozney Design, Inc.
Composition: Bookworks Plus
Printed in the United States of America
10  9  8  7  6  5  4  3  2

**Text Photo Credits**
Color photo graphics: J. Gerard Smith Photography
Page xvi: © The Image Bank/Douglas J. Fisher
Page 20: © Woodfin Camp & Associates, Inc./George Hall
Page 40: © The Stock Market
Page 60: © Photo Edit/Michael Newmans
Page 80: © UPI/Bettmann/Dann Pierce

# ABOUT THIS SERIES

*Careers without College* is designed to help those who don't have a four-year college degree (and don't plan on getting one any time soon) find a career that fits their interests, talents and personality. It's for you if you're about to choose your career—or if you're planning to change careers and don't want to invest a lot of time or money in more education or training, at least not right at the start.

Some of the jobs featured do require an associate degree; others only require on-the-job training that may take a year, some months or only a few weeks. In today's increasingly competitive job market, you may want to eventually consider getting a two- or maybe a four-year college degree in order to move up in a field.

Each title in the series features five jobs in a particular industry or career area. Some of them are "ordinary," others are glamorous. The competition to get into certain featured occupations is intense; as a balance, we have selected jobs under the same career umbrella that are easier to enter. Some of the other job opportunities within each field will be featured in future titles in this series.

*Careers without College* has up-to-date information that comes from extensive interviews with experts in each field. The format is designed for easy reading. Plus, each book gives you something unique: an insider look at the featured jobs through interviews with people who work in them now.

We invite your comments about the series, which will help us with future titles. Please send your correspondence to: Careers Without College, c/o Peterson's Guides, Inc., P.O. Box 2123, Princeton, NJ 08543-2123.

Peggy Schmidt has written about education and careers for twenty years. She is author of Peterson's best-selling *The 90-Minute Resume*.

# ABOUT THE AUTHOR

As a print media professional for many years, Linda Peterson is a generalist who knows a little about a lot of subjects. Now a freelance writer and editor, she began her career as a newspaper reporter and feature writer for the Gannett newspaper group, moving to King Features syndicate as a senior editor. She was on the articles staff at *Glamour* magazine and served as articles editor for *Ladies' Home Journal.* She has also done editing or writing for *Redbook, McCall's, Working Woman, Longevity,* and *First* magazines, and she writes a column for *Arts & Entertainment Monthly.* A native of Cleveland, she lives in Larchmont, New York.

# ACKNOWLEDGMENTS

Many thanks to the following people who helped provide sources and information, and made other contributions to this book. Several truly came through with "emergency services!"

Jacqui Anderson, Interlibrary loans, Larchmont Public Library, Larchmont, New York

Neale Baxter, Managing Editor, *Occupational Outlook Quarterly,* Bureau of Labor Statistics, Washington, D.C.

James Bothwell, Director of Operations, STAT, Pittsburgh, Pennsylvania

Maria Boza, Editor/Research Associate, Police Foundation, Washington, D.C.

Bill Brown, Director, National Registry of Emergency Medical Technicians, Columbus, Ohio

Sgt. John D. Clifford, Office of the Police Commissioner, New York City Police Department

Maria Conway, Manager, Human Resources, Metropolitan Emergency Medical Services, Little Rock, Arkansas

Penny Dechairo, Administrative Assistant, Emergency Care Information Center, Jems Communications, Carlsbad, California

Michele Dove, Research Assistant, International Association of Fire Fighters, Washington, D.C.

Kevin Duffy, Executive Director, APCO Institute, South Daytona, Florida

Sgt. Robert Faillaci, Stamford Police Department, Stamford, Connecticut

Fitch & Associates, Inc., and the Emergency Care Information Center, Jems Communications, for quotations from the 1992 JEMS Salary Survey, published in the November 1992 *Journal of Emergency Medical Services*

Patty Gerry, Public Affairs, National Fire Protection Association, Quincy, Massachusetts

Philip Gormley, Operations Director, Wilderness Medical Associates, Bryant Pond, Maine

Jack T. Grandey, EMT-P, Course Coordinator, Center for Emergency Medicine of Western Pennsylvania, Pittsburgh, Pennsylvania

Mary Harding, Mission Programs Director, National Association for Search and Rescue, Fairfax, Virginia

John Jones, Senior Fire Service Specialist, National Fire Protection Association, Quincy, Massachusetts

Lt. Marvin E. Jones, Director of Communications, Volusia County Sheriff's Department, Daytona Beach, Florida

Lt. Rick Kastigar, Pima County Sheriff's Department, Tucson, Arizona

Mark Lockhart, NREMT-P, President, National Association of Emergency Medical Technicians, Kansas City, Missouri

Capt. Patrick McMahon, Commanding Officer, Communications Division, Yonkers Police Department, Yonkers, New York

Bill Pierce, Chief Ranger, Olympic National Park, Port Angeles, Washington

Police Foundation, Washington, D.C., for material from its 1991 publication, *The Big Six: Policing America's Largest Cities*

Andrew Salvatore, retired police officer, New York City Police Department

Jerry Sanford, Office of Public Information, New York City Fire Department

Chase Sargent, Battalion Chief, Virginia Beach, Virginia, Fire Department

Volunteer Ambulance Corps, Town of Mamaroneck/Village of Larchmont, Mamaroneck, New York

Kirk Waggoner, Deputy Sheriff, Park County Sheriff's Department, Wyoming

Gail Zavatchan, NREMT-P, Lakewood Hospital Emergency Medical Service, Lakewood, Ohio

A special thanks for his endless help to F. Scott Romme, Vice President, Dive Rescue International, Inc., Fort Collins, Colorado. And to all the articulate, thoughtful people who took the time to fill out the author's questionnaires.

# WHAT'S IN THIS BOOK

# WHY THESE "EMERGENCY" CAREERS?

The world of emergency and protective services offers some of the most exciting and rewarding ways to make a living. These careers provide a clear sense of purpose and are guaranteed to make your adrenaline pump. That's because they're often high pressure and fast paced, and can involve life-threatening situations. You may have to rescue someone from a car accident or burning building, chase an armed lawbreaker, know instantly how to treat a trauma patient, or give clear instructions that will enable someone else to save a life.

These jobs are stressful because you may have to put your own safety on the line, and they can result in failure no matter how well you perform. But the rewards are enormous. Few other people, besides those in the medical profession, can have the satisfaction of knowing that their efforts saved another human being.

In this book you will find five emergency-related careers discussed in detail:

❏ Police officer

❏ Firefighter

❏ Emergency medical technician (EMT)

❏ Dispatcher

❏ Rescue specialist

Only those who genuinely like people and want to help them need apply, for the common theme here is "service." The careers selected for this book all demand employees who are dedicated to serving people in need.

These jobs are related in other ways. For example, a witness to a multiple car accident may telephone for help. A 911 or other emergency dispatcher answers the call. He or she then alerts the police, the ambulance service and its EMTs, and, most likely, a technical rescue team as well.

The good news for young people and career changers is that none of these occupations requires a college degree to get your foot in the door. If you are appointed to a police or fire department, you will receive your training at the city's police or fire academy over several months. Dispatch training may involve classroom instruction once you are hired, but it is typically done on-the-job over several weeks or months. Becoming an emergency medical technician requires the most education upfront: you'll need to be certified at the EMT-basic level before you can land a paying job. You can usually get this training in night classes at a community or junior college. They last about four months.

In addition to updated information about each of these careers, you will get a highly personal, "hands on" sense of them by reading the interviews at the end of every chapter. Three people who are doing the job tell you what it's really like and why they enjoy coming to work. One clue: they're rarely—if ever—bored. They prefer the unpredictable nature of each workday and the fact that no two calls for help are exactly the same. They also like being on the move and often working outdoors. Indeed, the only people who stay in one spot all day are the dispatchers—but they participate in the drama through their telephone headsets.

The very nature of these careers means that they aren't for everyone. Firefighters know they will have to brave flames; police officers know they may confront suspects who have weapons. Dispatchers know most every call means someone in distress; EMTs and rescue workers know they will see people die. If you want to be one of these workers, you'll need to decide what situations you are willing to face.

Before you begin learning about these careers, you may find a little inspiration by reading the tales of two heroes. For them, their deeds were all in a day's work. Then discover what the police commissioner of New York City, Raymond W. Kelly, has to tell young people about the chance to "make a difference" in their choice of career.

# RAYMOND W. KELLY

## on the Rewards of Serving the Public

As the new police commissioner for the city of New York, Raymond W. Kelly has the exciting challenge of running the world's largest police department.

He comes to that challenge with 29 years' experience on the force, along with a reputation, as a problem solver, a sure-handed manager and a master of detail. In addition to his "street smarts," he also brings the knowledge gained through many years of education. He earned a bachelor's degree from Manhattan College, a master's degree in public administration from

Harvard University, a law degree from St. John's University School of Law, and a master's in law from New York University Law School.

Commissioner Kelly, 51, began his career in the department as a cadet fresh from college and received the award for the highest grade in his police academy class. Shortly after joining the force, however, he left to serve for three years in the Marine Corps. On his return, he began a steady rise up the ranks. He was promoted to sergeant in 1969, lieutenant in 1974, captain in 1980, deputy inspector in 1984 and inspector in 1985, deputy chief in 1987 and assistant chief in 1988. He was named first deputy police commissioner in 1990, and was appointed to the top post in October 1992. During his uniformed career, he received 15 citations for meritorious performance, and one year was valedictorian of the department's Spanish language school.

Upon his appointment to commissioner, Kelly noted that his top priority was completing the establishment of the community policing program begun by his predecessor, Lee P. Brown.

More than 400 cities throughout the nation have moved to a community policing system, but none with a department as big as New York's. The concept is designed to put more officers on neighborhood foot patrol, getting to know the people in their community. It places more emphasis on problem solving and less on simply making arrests and moving on to the next emergency radio call. The program will build the department to the unprecedented level of 32,000 uniformed officers by 1996.

That means recruitment, recruitment and more recruitment. To spread the word about the rewards of policing in general and the New York City Police Department in particular, Commissioner Kelly accepted the offer to talk to *Emergencies* readers about his favorite subject.


I have loved this business since I first set foot in it. I was working as a stock boy at Macy's when I saw an advertisement for the police cadet program for college students, which was similar to the program we have now. I joined the department as a cadet. They gave us some training and sent us out to do essentially clerical tasks. My first job was answering the switchboard.

I remember that the job exposed me for the first time to the pulse and vibrancy of the city. The switchboard was at an administrative control center, so we didn't have too many emergency calls. But whatever was going on in the police department, the information was coming in there. It was kind of exciting for a young person like me to be exposed to it, and as a result, I really did fall in love with policing.

I really enjoyed patrol, being the "face" of the police department. I liked either walking a beat or riding in a radio car. I hated to get out of the radio car at the end of the day, especially after a busy tour. Every day is different for police officers. They run into different people, have different experiences. Whenever I can, I still go and sit in the back of a police car and ride around and answer the assignments with the officers because I just find it exciting.

Of course, there are things that are upsetting, too; obviously some days are better than others. From my earlier years, I can remember certain incidents, like being with a ten-year-old boy who'd been hit by a coal truck. I was under the truck with him, talking to him, trying to keep him calm. He was barely alive and he later died. That type of thing sticks with you. I also was in Youth Division for awhile, and I used to go in and see kids who were neglected or abused. The conditions that they lived in were really depressing. On those days, you have a lot of mixed feelings. You feel helpless, you sometimes feel maybe you should be making a living another way.

But what always made me go back the next day was the feeling that I could make a difference, that I could do some good. I loved the ability to help people. That probably sounds corny, but it really is a rewarding experience to help people.

When I was patrolling the street I could see that if you have any communication with people, the barriers come down fairly quickly. That's what we're trying to do now, and that's what's happening with community policing. We're not the only ones involved in it; other major cities throughout the country are doing it, too. It's not a program as much as it's a philosophy, an approach to life. I think it's working. We're getting a lot of positive feedback coming back to the department.

People have asked me what makes a good police officer. Probably the three most important traits a good cop needs to have are compassion, a sense of humor and just generally good character. You have to have your own set of values. We have a lot of "public values" here, but I think you have to have your own sense of personal integrity.

I think police work—or any of the other careers in this book—tends to attract a certain type of person: someone who enjoys helping others and finds it very rewarding. I think most police officers do. They don't always say that, but I think, down deep, that's why most people come into policing, and that's probably the same motivation for the fire department or EMS or dispatch. So I'd encourage young people to consider them all, because I think, quite frankly, that not everybody is cut out to be a police officer.

We're always looking for talented people, and I think we offer very good jobs for those who don't yet have a four-year degree. And it's easier now than ever before to continue your college education once you're in the department. We have an increasing number of scholarships and partial scholarships, and we encourage it for promotion, so it's sort of a self-supporting concept. To become a sergeant you need 64 credits; to become a captain, you must have a four-year degree. Most of the people who are above the rank of captain have some sort of graduate degree.

I'd also like to encourage women and minority candidates who wonder if police work might be right for them. Our department doesn't properly reflect the population of this city as far as minorities and women are concerned, and we're looking for more. We have a long way to go in that regard, and I think we clearly are an equal opportunity employer. We certainly want to put out the message that this is a welcoming and friendly environment.

I know that parents sometimes worry that police work is too dangerous and may try to dissuade their children from going into it. Yet the vast majority of work performed by officers is in the service area. There is some risk, but it is relatively small. There's always going to be some risk;

LIFE is a risk. But I think the job satisfaction you get far outweighs the risk factor.

Traditionally, we've always focused on people making police work a vocation for the rest of their working lives. But maybe today you might think about coming in for a couple years and then going on to other things. If it's not for you, well, the department will have made some friends, people who know what it's all about to be a police officer. And that's important, because through the years police have been isolated. They tend to become a self-insulating group—the "us against them; only we know what we do" type of approach. Having more people who can relate to the police experience can help change that.

If you're thinking about a career in the police department, even if you're just remotely interested, I'd suggest that you start the process rolling because it can be a pretty protracted one. It takes us almost two years to hire someone, though we're trying to cut that down substantially. We're hiring so many people right now that we can't hire them quickly enough.

We'll be hiring almost 9,000 cops between now and the end of 1995. To get that number, we have to process a lot of people. We have a medical exam, a psychological exam, a character investigation; there's a lot of work to be done. Much of the process is driven by the individual, who has to supply names of references, a driver's license, etc. The candidate needs to have things in order.

If you look at police work with an objective eye, you'll find that it's a great job in terms of salary and benefits compared to what's out there in the private sector. But much more than that, it's a real opportunity to make a difference, not to be a sideline sitter, not to watch the world on the 10 o'clock news, but to actually participate in making things change for the better. And you really do get that sense that you're doing something meaningful and making life better for people.

Policing is a real rewarding job. You're never going to have a lot of money, but you are going to be rich in other ways.

# A SALUTE TO TWO HEROES

A pat on the back to two people who truly know what these emergency careers are all about and why they can be so rewarding.

**Pat Everett, 36, Dispatcher, Federal Way Fire Department, Federal Way, Washington**

"I knew I'd found my niche," Pat Everett says, recalling the time ten years ago when she began her first job as a dispatcher. She's been proving it ever since, but never more so than she did on November 21, 1991.

That morning, Everett took a 911 call from a hysterical mother: her 13-month-old baby had drowned in the bathtub when she'd briefly left the room. Everett coached the frantic woman on how to give the baby CPR (cardiopulmonary resuscitation) and pushed her to keep going and not give up until the fire department rescuers arrived minutes later.

After a hospital stay, the baby recovered completely. His grateful parents still bring him to visit the dispatcher who helped save his life. "They've thanked me many, many times," says Everett.

That event and another involving Pat Everett have been featured on the television program *Rescue 911*.

**Rick Neumann, 37, Fire Apparatus Operator, Heavy Rescue Unit, Squad 52, Cincinnati Fire Department, Cincinnati, Ohio**

On a July midnight in 1992, a family stunned by a tragic drowning was saved from a second loss by Rick Neumann's quick action.

As firefighters were pulling the drowned man's body from the Ohio River onto a boat dock, his distraught wife broke away from those comforting her and bolted toward the river. "I saw her running, and I knew she was headed for the water," Neumann recalls. "I ran and hit the water about the same time she did. I swam over and grabbed her. The river bank was dredged out, so it was all mud and very steep. I couldn't pull her up out of the water by myself. I stuck my hand in the mud to hold us both in place until the others put down a ladder for us to climb out."

Neumann received a commendation for his efforts as did his fellow firefighters for their attempts to revive the woman's husband.

**Television shows often dramatize the adventure and danger of a police officer's job— chasing criminals, foiling a robbery, stopping the drug trade. But even though there can be high-stakes action, a typical day's work involves much more than "getting the bad guys." Many officers spend most of their time providing service, information and problem-solving for the law-abiding citizens of the community they patrol.**

P olice officers provide a sense of safety, whether they're enforcing society's rules of behavior or the laws of traffic. The task of sworn police officers—those authorized to carry guns and make arrests—is to prevent crime, maintain the peace and arrest lawbreakers.

1

Though police may work for county, state and federal governments, their most familiar role is as the municipal police officer—the "cop on the beat." In rural areas, the sheriff's department is generally responsible for law and order, in addition to its regular duty of maintaining the county jail and safeguarding the courts.

Although many days are uneventful and routine, that can change in a moment. In the course of their duties, police officers are more likely to encounter dangerous people than almost any other workers. As a result, a cop's tools of the trade are many and potentially deadly. Police work with handguns, rifles, shotguns and tear gas. They carry handcuffs, a nightstick, and may sometimes wear a bulletproof vest or a riot helmet.

Who's qualified for this unique job? Typically, police recruits must be U.S. citizens, high school graduates, and no younger than 19 (20 or 21 in some areas) nor older than 29 (or up to 35 in some areas) before they apply. They cannot have been convicted of a felony crime or dishonorably discharged from military service.

If you want to become a police officer, you usually must pass many exams—written, medical and psychological—including a lie detector exam and drug testing. Your personal background and general character will also be investigated. If you pass muster and are appointed to a police department, you will attend formal training at a police academy for several months (unless you work for a very small department).

In some cities, college students are hired as police cadets or trainees, doing clerical tasks while they study law enforcement. Usually, they join the force when they are 21. Becoming a volunteer "auxiliary" or reserve officer also may lead to a full-time job, though it's not a typical route. Some departments have a ride-along program in which interested persons can accompany police officers during routine shifts. Such exposure could help some people assess whether this really is the job they want.

As New York City Police Commissioner Raymond Kelly observed at the start of this book, the career of the police officer is not for everyone. But if you sincerely want to be one of those who can answer the public's many calls for help, it may well be the career for you.

## What You Need to Know

❏ Driver's training and techniques (to pursue speeding motorists and criminal suspects)
❏ State and local laws
❏ Police science
❏ The legal rights of accused persons
❏ Techniques of directing traffic

## Necessary Skills

❏ How to conduct an investigation of an accident, crime or other incident
❏ Good verbal skills to communicate with the public and with co-workers
❏ Neatness, good penmanship for written reports
❏ How to use firearms
❏ How to give first aid
❏ Self-defense techniques

## Do You Have What It Takes?

❏ Honesty and integrity
❏ Self-confidence (you have to come across as the person in charge)
❏ Even temperament (even ordinary citizens can strain your patience)
❏ Dependability (particularly crucial in small departments)
❏ Good judgment, common sense
❏ Keen powers of observation
❏ Ability to stay calm in tense situations
❏ Ability to think and act quickly
❏ Sensitivity to different types of people
❏ An ability to persuade people to get the desired results (i.e. talking before "strong-arming" them)
❏ Willingness to work weekends, holidays and rotating shifts
❏ Desire to work with people and serve the public
❏ Sense of humor

**◆ Getting into the Field**

3

*Physical Attributes*

- ❑ Manual dexterity to use firearms
- ❑ Excellent health, physical stamina
- ❑ 20/20 eyesight generally required (many departments permit corrective lenses) and no color blindness
- ❑ Normal hearing in both ears
- ❑ Weight in proportion to height

*Education*

Virtually all police departments require candidates to have a high school diploma or a GED (general equivalency diploma). An associate degree in criminal justice may be a plus in landing a job. The ability to speak a foreign language also may be helpful in getting hired, especially in cities that have highly diverse ethnic populations.

*Licenses Required*

Driver's license

**Job Outlook**

**Competition for jobs:** very competitive

Because of the good pay and benefits, there usually are more qualified applicants for police work than there are openings. Local and state government budgets—and cutbacks in them—are a primary factor in the number of jobs available. Though there is expected to be an increasing demand for police services throughout the nineties, a city's finances will affect its ability to hire extra officers.

**The Ground Floor**

**Entry-level job:** probationary officer or "rookie"

New graduates of the police academy typically start out on patrol. They either ride alone or with a partner in a marked police car, or walk the streets on foot patrol.

Both new and veteran police officers generally perform the same tasks, although the rookie is closely guided by a superior officer during the probation period. The main difference in duties depends on the size of the department. In a big city, an officer is likely to concentrate on either patrol or traffic duty, while the small-town officer may wear many hats.

Officers report to the station house on the car's police radio or from police call boxes or telephones at regular intervals. On the police radio, many police departments have their own language—a number system that saves time. For example, a car accident is a "10-53"; an officer who needs help fast is a "10-13."

### *Entry-level and Experienced Officers*

❑ Patrol assigned area ("beat" or "sector") in marked police car, on foot or (in some areas) on motorcycle

❑ Respond to 911 calls or other assignments given over the police radio

❑ Look out for suspicious persons or circumstances, such as lights in empty buildings

❑ Investigate accidents

❑ Give first aid to accident victims or other injured persons

❑ Direct traffic around fires, accidents or other emergency situations

❑ Enforce traffic laws and issue tickets to violators

❑ Control crowds at public gatherings

❑ Warn or arrest persons who violate laws and ordinances

❑ Keep a log of the day's events and file written reports with the superior officer

❑ When necessary, testify in court in criminal cases following an arrest

## ◆ On-the-Job Responsi-bilities

## When You'll Work

Police work is never a nine-to-five job, as society must be protected 24 hours a day. Though most officers average a 40-hour week, schedules vary. Typically, most officers work eight-hour shifts that rotate on a weekly, monthly or quarterly basis. A day shift might be 7 A.M. to 3 P.M.; the afternoon shift 3 P.M. to 11 P.M.; and the night shift 11 P.M. to 7 A.M. Some cops may work five days straight and get two days off; others may work four ten-hour days and get three off.

Such constant change, especially when shifts rotate weekly, can be very hard on the body's sleep-wake cycle as well as on family needs and routines. As a result, an increasing number of police departments are allowing officers to choose "steady tour," in which they work the same shift all the time.

## Time Off

Entry-level officers generally receive at least ten days vacation, though some departments are more generous. For example, the Chicago, Detroit and New York City police departments offer 20 days vacation to start. Seniority usually determines the choice of weeks taken.

All major holidays are observed. Those officers who must be on duty generally are paid double time. Paid sick days are liberal in number.

## Perks

❏ Generous medical and insurance benefits
❏ Typically, some college tuition paid for law enforcement studies, and there may be higher pay when an associate or bachelor's degree is earned
❏ Option of early retirement at half-pay (typically after 20 to 25 years of service)
❏ Guns, handcuffs and other required equipment is typically provided, along with uniforms or a cash allowance toward uniforms
❏ On occasion, the chance to meet celebrities while providing security

❑ Municipal police departments (cities, towns and villages)
❑ County police and sheriff's departments
❑ State police departments
❑ Federal agencies such as the U.S. Park Police

**Entry-level and experienced officers:** little potential for travel.

At one time or another, most police officers go for new or refresher training at a facility other than their local department.

Police officers usually work outdoors, walking or driving in all kinds of weather—on hot, humid days or in the bitter cold. The "view" depends on the beat. Cops may patrol wealthy residential areas or tenement housing, modern office complexes or rundown industrial areas, downtown commercial districts or suburban shopping malls.

The precinct's police station itself might be new, spacious and nicely decorated or old, cramped and furnished with drab "government-issue" equipment. Generally, there are many officers' desks in a single room, a high noise level from people and telephones and little privacy.

❑ Potential for medical problems related to high stress
❑ Threat of exposure to infectious diseases, including the AIDS virus, while giving a bleeding accident victim first aid or other emergency treatment
❑ Misery for allergy sufferers in hay fever season (for those who are outdoors)

There is tremendous range in police officers' pay, depending on the size of the department, the region and an individual's level of experience.

According to the 1992 edition of the *Municipal Year Book*'s survey of 1,452 cities, the average starting salary for all police officers was $23,474. The maximum was

$30,881 for officers who have not been promoted to sergeant. Officers regularly receive raises until they reach the maximum pay rate for their rank.

Large cities tend to pay higher salaries. In New York City, for example, rookies start at $28,748 and earn $48,827 after five years. Overall, salaries are somewhat higher in the West, especially California, and they are lower in the South.

When officers work overtime—which may be often—they generally are paid at a rate of time-and-a-half, although some departments may compensate them in time off instead. Holidays often are paid at double time. There also may be an extra "differential" for working the afternoon or night shift. In addition, some departments provide extra "longevity pay" to officers who have served at least six years.

Many police officers are represented by a union such as the Patrolmen's Benevolent Association or the Fraternal Order of Police. The union negotiates their salaries and benefits.

## Moving Up

After rookies complete their period of probation—anywhere from six months to three years—they become eligible for promotion. To move up to the ranks to sergeant, lieutenant and captain generally means scoring highly on written civil service exams and having excellent on-the-job performance. Plainclothes detectives generally are appointed on merit. Further promotion often requires a bachelor's degree or even a master's. Awards and citations for bravery in the line of duty or other special honors help in advancement.

Many officers choose to remain on regular patrol throughout their careers. Some, especially in large departments, make lateral moves into specialty units such as drug enforcement, mounted patrol, youth services, criminal laboratory sciences or community relations.

Most of the estimated 530,000 full-time police officers in the United States work for local and state police departments, of which there are approximately 17,000. By far the largest department is New York City, which employs 28,600 uniformed officers to protect its nearly 8 million residents. Chicago, the next largest department, has less than half that many police officers. Other major departments include Los Angeles; Philadelphia; Houston; Washington, D.C.; Detroit; Baltimore; Dallas; San Diego; and San Antonio. A mid-size city might have several hundred police officers, while hundreds of small communities may employ fewer than 25.

◆ **Where the Jobs Are**

Virtually all recruits newly appointed by a police department begin their training at the city's police academy. Typically, over the next four to six months, recruits study law, police science and social science.

◆ **Training**

It is here that they learn such things as how to use guns, the laws of their city and state, constitutional law and an individual's civil rights, self-defense techniques, how to drive a patrol car, how to give first aid, the tactics of crowd control and how to investigate an accident.

At the end of training, the recruits usually must take a written exam and give a practical demonstration of their skills. If they pass, they are formally issued their badge, shield and gun and they are assigned to a police station.

The nation's first official sworn policewoman assumed her duties in Los Angeles in 1910. But it wasn't until the 1970s that the number of women in law enforcement really began to grow. Still, most police departments are overwhelmingly male: a 1991 federal survey found that 10.3 percent of all public-service police officers and detectives are women. In New York City, women account for 14 percent of the uniformed police force.

Although the first women officers generally were lim-

◆ **The Male/Female Equation**

ited to duties such as handling female offenders or writing parking tickets, today's policewomen serve in all divisions of a department.

## Making Your Decision: What to Consider

**The Bad News**

❏ Daily threat of personal injury or loss of life
❏ Rotating shifts and holiday/evening work that can be hard on officers and their families
❏ Personal liability—the risk of civil lawsuits or departmental punishment
❏ Working outdoors in all kinds of weather
❏ Potential for health problems related to stress

**The Good News**

❏ Challenging work with much responsibility
❏ Satisfaction of helping people in need
❏ Never the same job every day (no two calls are alike)
❏ Strong job security and good benefits
❏ Pride in capturing lawbreakers and bringing criminals to justice

## More Information Please

First go to the source: your municipal police department will provide entrance information. In large cities the police may have a central personnel office or recruitment section. Information on preliminary requirements and dates for entry exams can also be obtained from the city or state's Civil Service Commission (often listed in a telephone directory's "Blue Pages" of government offices.)

Updated information about the salaries, work hours and size of the police force in several hundred cities is published annually by the International City Management Association in the *Municipal Year Book,* which can be found in many public libraries.

**WHAT IT'S REALLY LIKE**

**Kim Shea**, 30,
police officer,
New York City Police Department,
Precinct 52, North Bronx
Years on the force: five

**Why did you decide to become a police officer?**
My brother is a cop, and he encouraged me to think about
it. He loves the job and thought I would, too, especially
since I had some paralegal background. So I took the (civil
service) test in October '86 and got called in January '87. I
started police academy that summer.

**What was police academy training like?**
It was grueling! For six months I had no life. You had to be
there at seven in the morning—no excuses. It was in July,
boiling hot, and we had to run two to five miles every day.
We also had two and a half hours of gym—weightlifting,
self-defense, calisthenics. I'm 5 feet 6 inches tall and
weighed 128 pounds, and I did pretty well. Also, we had to
take law, social science and police science classes daily.
Actually, I loved it.

**What was your first job after graduating from the academy?**

In January, I was assigned foot patrol in the Midtown South and North precincts—the busiest in the city. It includes 42nd Street, the Port Authority, lots of traffic and sightseers. I worked by myself from 6 P.M. to 2 A.M. It was an adventure every day.

When the temperature was below freezing we were supposed to get the homeless people off the street and to a shelter. On one shift I remember going up to one homeless guy sleeping huddled in a blanket. I said, "Sir? Sir?" and all of a sudden he just threw that blanket off and lunged at me—I almost jumped out of my skin! I called for another unit to give me a hand. He was acting violent, saying "Get away!" although eventually he calmed down, picked up his belongings and left. You have to watch out for them; they can be the nicest people, or they can be crazy.

**What was the hardest aspect of the job at the start?**

Being out in the elements all the time. It was absolutely freezing on foot patrol in January. And I was there until July, so I was either freezing or sweating!

**What other jobs have you held?**

After my six months of field training, I left Midtown and went to BAND—Bronx Anti-Narcotics Drive. They pick a spot in the precinct that's real bad with drugs, and they put a cop on every corner. It's meant to send a message to the drug dealers. We try to flood their area to get the drugs out of the streets, out of the lobbies, out of the cars. My purpose was to arrest anyone with any drug—one crack vial, one joint, one hypo (needle), anything—where normally they would only get a summons.

I stayed with BAND for a year until the unit was dissolved. Then I went into a regular squad, and that's what I'm in now. I drive the patrol sergeant—he's in charge of all the police officers on patrol. We're always on the road, covering the entire precinct. I work 4 P.M. to midnight all the time.

**How long did it take before you felt "established" on the job?**
Probably about four years. I generally felt pretty confident, set, ready, I understood everything; I was in my routine.

**Did you ever feel there was more pressure on you because you're a woman?**
Yes. You don't want to say or do anything stupid, and you're more likely to be looked at to do something stupid! But any rookie has to prove himself or herself, and there comes a point when you know the guys trust you. You hear them say about someone, "She's a great cop" or "She really deserved that detail (special assignment)." It feels good when you hear them say it—you're always looking for your peers' acceptance.

**What do you like most about your work?**
I love to see how people live. In our precinct we have a real melting pot of different cultures. There are also a lot of elderly people. My grandmother lived in our precinct. I loved seeing her and her friends on the bench at the park every day. I love to see the families, the children.

Not that it's all good, of course, because it's not. Especially when we get involved with the BCW cases (Bureau of Child Welfare). We just had a case, with four kids, the mother beat them with a wire hanger. The oldest was only four, but he took care of the others. He told me, "My sister needs a bottle, my sister needs a diaper change." He knew everything. He said, "My mama beat me because I forgot how old I was."

**What do you like least about your work?**
Well, the kind of thing I just mentioned is tough to see. And there's always the violence. Last night a guy got shot in the head; it was an old, ongoing dispute over a girl. His family came to the hospital, and the doctors told them he was going to be paralyzed. It's just heartbreaking to see the pain on these people's faces.

**What advice would you give someone who's considering a career as a police officer?**
Are you going to take the career seriously? Or are you just looking for a 20-year job so you can get the pension and leave? And you'd better have a very long fuse. It had better

13

be three blocks long because you've got to put up with so much.

But I love my job. I wouldn't trade it for the world. Every day is different. You don't know where you're going to be or what you're going to be doing.

## **Steven Gaughan,** 27,
## police officer,
## Prince Georges County Police Department,
## District 3, Landover, Maryland
## Years on the force: three

**How did you get into police work?**
My father was a Boston cop for 34 years, and that's what I wanted to be. I was working in a supermarket while I tried for Boston (police department) on a number of occasions. I was getting 97's and 98's on the civil service test but that wasn't good enough—they had umpteen thousands of people taking the test. So I started applying elsewhere, to California and Florida. It was just by luck I came down here. My uncle said they were hiring and sent me an application.

**What was police academy like?**
I'd been in the National Guard, and the first few days were kind of like military basic training. I thought it was a little easier than I expected.

The training lasted six months. I think we started with vehicle law, then criminal law. You spend about a month and a half just in law. They go over pretty much everything you need to know as a patrolman—everything you can make arrests on, what can and can't be done, what's a crime, what isn't.

You're also taught human relations, how to deal with people. If you know how to use your mouth you don't have to use force. They teach you how to do building entries, how to respond to a domestic (dispute). They're the most dangerous calls because you never really know what's going to go off. People don't like you coming into their house and telling them what's going on. Sometimes on domestics they expect us to come and in 10 or 15 minutes solve the problems that they've been having for years.

**What was the most difficult part of the job at first?**
Coming from Boston and not knowing the area I had a hard time getting around. And in general, learning how to deal with the people and what to look for. When I first came on I rode for 14 weeks with an FTO—a field training officer. I remember the first time we pulled up on a drug deal. Before I knew it he had three guys on the ground, he had his gun out, and I was, like, I didn't know what was going on. There's the textbook, and then there's real life. It was quite an experience that first day.

**How long was it before you felt confident?**
Probably a month after being on my own. Before that I think I relied on the FTO too much to help me out. But once you're on your own, you're on your own.

**What is a typical day like for you?**
You'll go in and have roll call for 10 to 15 minutes. They'll tell you everything that's going on in your area, lookouts for people who are wanted. After that you'll go to your beat, handle 911 calls, answer domestic calls. Some cops do traffic stops and shoot radar (use radar guns to catch speeders).

Usually another guy and I hook up and go to the high drug areas. My goal is (to get into) vice. What I want is a street-level kind of vice like the "jump outs" you see on TV. That's why I key so much on drug arrests. When I go for my interview for vice, they'll ask how many drug arrests I've had.

**What do you like most about your work?**
I like the excitement. I think that's why I took it. And it's different every day; it's not the same old nine-to-five thing. On some calls it's a real rush of adrenaline, it's a good feeling. We'll get a call about a beating in progress and a lot of guys will race to it because they want to get that bad guy.

**What do you like least?**
That's easy. Paperwork. For every arrest you make, you have to do a lot of reports. A drug arrest takes about three and a half hours.

**What accomplishments are you most proud of so far?**
Working with the kids. We go to a school a couple of times a week for a mentor program; about six or seven of us do it. The program assigns each of us one or two kids, problem kids, and we see if we can straighten them out. They're usually third and fourth graders from single-parent homes.

We take them to a wrestling match, we take them to a park—just do stuff with them in general. Last year I did it, and it felt good that "my" kid started getting all A's. One of the mothers wrote the (police) chief a letter saying how much her kid had improved and that he was now in the "Excel" program. Once I started doing it, it was a lot of fun.

**What advice would you give someone considering police work?**
Go for it. I really enjoy the job and can't see myself doing anything else.

## Debra A. Guidet, 39, detective/firefighter, Department of Public Safety, Rohnert Park, California Years on the force: ten

**How did you get interested in police work?**
I was living down in Mojave, finishing my associate degree in liberal arts. There was an opening for a police and fire dispatcher in nearby California City, so I applied. I was hired and trained on the job. I did that for about ten months and discovered I really loved the police aspect of the work.

At the time that I decided I wanted to be a police officer women were generally not being accepted unless they were the "Amazon-type." I was 5 feet 1 inch and weighed 98 pounds, and a lot of people were telling me I was crazy. But I'm a living example that if you want something bad enough you can work hard and get it.

**So how did you break into the field?**
I moved back to the area where I grew up and became a

dispatcher with the Petaluma police department. I was also studying for another associate degree, this time in administration of justice.

I left dispatch to develop a bicycle safety education program for Petaluma and its schools under a federal grant. When that was over, I moved into a civilian position at the department as a community service officer. I took minor reports, did photo lab duties and controlled property/ evidence. Then I got a similar civilian job at the Santa Rosa police department as a police field technician. We answered nonemergency calls and assisted at crime scenes.

After that, I became a reserve police officer with another department, working at least 16 hours a month with a regular officer. I had also started taking the police entrance exams. They consisted of written, psychological and physical agility tests, and a full medical and background check. I took the exams for three cities and for a sheriff's department. I was passing the physical agility tests but I still wasn't getting hired.

When I turned 29, I knew my age was going to become a factor in my being hired. So I made the decision to pay my own way through the police academy. They accept a certain number of civilians.

**Did you have to pass an entrance exam?**
Oh yes. Everyone had to climb a six-foot wall, run an obstacle course, go over a balance beam, drag a 160-pound dummy about 25 yards, then pick it up and lift it onto a two-foot-high table. But I just could not lift that dummy.

I'd already waited a year to get into the academy, but I asked them if they'd hold my spot and let me try again later. They were surprised, but they agreed. For six months I did strength training. Then I came back, took the entrance test, passed it and got in!

The academy training took four months and cost me about $400. After I graduated in December '81, I applied like mad for a job. In March of '82, I was hired by Rohnert Park as their first female public safety officer.

**Is that different from a "regular" police officer?**
Yes, because in our city a public safety officer is both a
police officer and a firefighter. Ninety percent of the time
we're police. There are 40 officers serving a city of 40,000,
so we depend a lot on our volunteer firefighters. We also
get to keep our patrol cars on a 24-hour basis, mainly because all our fire gear is in the car.

I got my fire training on the job. When I first got hired I
thought, come on, I'm very petite, I know my limitations.
But the chief said, "We do a team effort here and that's
what gets us through. Nobody goes in by him or herself."

**As the first woman on the force, did you ever
feel unwelcome?**
Never. Not even in the firefighting. These guys are really
great—they're the first ones to pitch in and ask if you need
help. As long as you—or anyone else—are doing your best
and giving 100 percent, you don't get any second looks.
Not many women want to be both firefighter and police
officer fulltime, though. I remained the department's first
and only female sworn officer until last year, when another
one was hired.

At the start, I remember the talk my chief had with me
about having to prove myself. He said, "Y'know, Deb,
once you roll around in the dirt with a guy (suspect), we'll
know you're going to be a good cop." Well, ten years later,
I've never had to get down in the dirt with a guy. My attrib-
ute is being able to talk to people, treating them just like
I'd want to be treated. Generally I can communicate with
people well enough to not have to get physical.

**So how do all the hats you wear work out on a given
day?**
If I'm on duty and we have a major structure fire, I'll put
on my fire gear and get on the fire truck. Then after the
fire is out I go home, take a shower, put on my police gear
and come back to work as a police officer. When I'm off
duty I have a beeper that goes off when there's a fire and it
tells me which battalion needs to respond. Now I'm classi-
fied as a fire engineer; I drive the fire truck.

**What did you do on your first job?**
I was on patrol. I spent six months in field training, learning how the city functions and how we do our job here. I drove by myself, and each day I usually had a different beat. There are four beats here, and they moved us around.

**How did you become a detective?**
In my five years on patrol, I realized that I wanted to specialize. I'd already been taking classes on my own, in juvenile and sexual assault investigation. So if they (detectives) felt that they needed somebody to assist in a major case investigation of rape or sexual assault, I went out on my own time. I knew it could help to have a woman to assist if she (the victim) was not comfortable talking to a man.

One Friday my lieutenant called me at home—and told me to report on Monday to the detective's division. He said they needed help with child abuse and sexual assault cases. I've been a detective for five years now, specializing in those areas. I work 8 A.M. to 4 P.M. every day.

**What do you like most about your work?**
Getting a conviction or a plea. The major satisfaction is when I can take the victim to the sentencing hearing. Before the judge passes sentence on the perpetrator, sometimes the victims are allowed to tell the judge how this (crime) has affected their lives. It never fails to bring me to tears. Finally it's over, and the family can get on with their lives.

**What do you like the least about your work?**
The crimes that I can't prove, even though we know a child has been abused. Those are the kind of cases that have you waking up in the middle of the night, thinking, "Did I forget to do something?"

**What advice would you give to someone who's thinking about becoming a police officer?**
Take classes to understand what law enforcement's about. You should understand the difficulty police officers have in society now, the restraints we have to work under. If you can, become a reserve officer. See if you like it. You've got to like what you're doing, especially in this kind of work, or you just don't last.

**When the fire alarm sounds, a rush of adrenaline sends firefighters scrambling into their protective uniforms and out to their trucks. What awaits them at the end of the ride could range from a smoking barbecue to a high-rise apartment blaze, to an overturned fuel truck on the interstate. They are modern heroes and heroines, risking their own lives to save others and to minimize property damage.**

Firefighters are organized into companies, each led by a commanding officer. The engine company has the pumper truck, which carries all the hoses. The ladder company has the truck with the "cherrypicker" tower ladder and/or an aerial ladder of 55 to 110 feet. Usually there are four firefighters

21

on the engine and five on the ladder truck, although many departments have less staffing.

At the scene of a fire teamwork is the rule. The engine crews attach hoses to fire hydrants, stretch the hoses into the burning structure and direct water onto the fire. The ladder crews use forcible entry tools to get into a structure and search for trapped victims. They also break windows or cut through the roof with an ax or chain saw to vent the building so the heat and smoke can escape. Any firefighter can perform any task, though, and when the fire is finally out, everybody does overhaul, the clean-up work that ensures the fire will not re-ignite.

Many departments also have a rescue company that carries special emergency equipment for freeing people from tangled car wrecks, or to fight marine fires (on ships and piers). Many also have special ''hazmat'' units trained to deal with spilled or burning hazardous materials such as chemicals. Firefighting has become a science, not just a simple matter of ''surround and drown.''

Although putting out fires is the most obvious part of the job, there are others. Calls for emergency medical service comprise the majority of calls to the nation's fire departments. Firefighters also try to prevent fires by educating the public through school and civic fire safety programs. They inspect buildings for unsafe conditions that could cause a fire, such as improper storage of flammable materials. They check that the fire exits are not blocked, and that fire alarms and sprinklers are working correctly.

Firefighting is a demanding job, but there are plenty of people who want to do it. Candidates generally must be between 18 and 35 years of age, United States citizens, and, in many cases, residents of the community they wish to serve. Some fire departments require that their members be nonsmokers. Candidates cannot have been dishonorably discharged from military service or have been convicted of a felony crime.

Firefighters are ordinary people, willing and able to do extraordinary things. They know danger waits on every call, and the shared experience forges a strong bond. If the challenge and the teamwork appeal to you, and you're physically capable, you may be an ideal candidate for the job.

## What You Need to Know

- ❏ The science of fire; how it travels
- ❏ Firefighting techniques, water hydraulics
- ❏ The nature of hazardous materials and chemicals
- ❏ Local fire and building codes
- ❏ Different types of building construction (frame, brick, steel, etc.)

## Necessary Skills

- ❏ How to give first aid and other emergency medical procedures such as CPR (a set of skills that can revive a person who has stopped breathing or whose heart has stopped)
- ❏ How to use ladders and hoses
- ❏ How to use axes, saws and special tools
- ❏ Methods of forcing entry into a burning structure
- ❏ Search and rescue techniques
- ❏ Mechanical aptitude

## Do You Have What It Takes?

- ❏ Courage to face life-threatening situations
- ❏ Common sense, good judgment
- ❏ Dependability
- ❏ Ability to work as a team member
- ❏ Ability to obey orders and trust another person's judgment
- ❏ Ability to function well under great stress and in adverse environments
- ❏ Congenial temperament (firefighters spend many hours with their colleagues)
- ❏ Good communication skills (to quickly give concise information or instructions about a fire, talk over the radio, write reports)

## Physical Attributes

- ❏ Good vision (correction to 20/30 with glasses or contact lenses generally permitted)

◆ **Getting into the Field**

❑ Normal hearing

❑ Manual dexterity to use tools and firefighting equipment

❑ Nimble fingers to quickly tie the correct knots in ropes

❑ Eye-hand-foot coordination to climb ladders while carrying equipment

In addition to the above, strength and great stamina are required of firefighters. They often must engage in heavy labor for several hours at a time while wearing protective clothing and an air pack that add many pounds of weight. They have to lift and carry ropes or hoses that can weigh 100 pounds or more while climbing ladders or running up stairs. The firefighter handling the hose nozzle must be strong enough to control and direct it as a tremendous force of water comes out.

Firefighters also must be agile, as the job involves a great deal of kneeling, bending and crouching. Good aerobic conditioning is also important because labored breathing can cause a firefighter to use up the 30-minutes' worth of air in the breathing apparatus more quickly.

The physical demands of the job are reflected in the physical ability entry test required of all potential recruits. A typical test may include such tasks as carrying 50 pounds of hose up several flights of stairs in a specified time; carrying or dragging a dummy weighing 125 pounds or more for 100 feet; climbing or vaulting over a wall that may be five to eight feet tall; picking up a ladder from the ground, raising it against a wall and securing it; and quickly pulling a hose or a heavy weight hand-over-hand up the side of a building.

### Education

A high school diploma is generally required. Helpful subjects include chemistry, physics, math, "shop," technical drawing and blueprint reading. Community college courses in fire science are a plus, as is emergency medical training, military service or the ability to speak another language. Construction industry workers also have experience that can be valuable in firefighting.

### *Licenses Required*

Driver's license

**Competition for jobs:** very competitive
Many people do not realize that the vast majority of the nation's estimated 1.6 million firefighters are volunteers. Only about 280,000 are career firefighters, of whom approximately 90 percent work for municipal fire departments.

In most areas, there are typically many more qualified applicants than job openings. That's mainly because getting in requires only a high school diploma, the salary and benefits are above average and the job itself is exciting.

There will be a greater need for firefighters as the population grows and suburban communities expand, but local government spending will restrict the number of new jobs. Also, employee turnover is fairly low.

Though employment processes vary greatly, some departments may be hiring under an affirmative action program—voluntary or court-ordered—in an effort to increase the number of women and minority firefighters. The testing process may be weighted in some manner to give preference to these candidates.

**Entry-level job:** probationary firefighter ("proby")
Both new hires and experienced firefighters essentially do the same job, though a proby is carefully supervised. At the scene of a fire, a new hire is less likely than a veteran to make the first entry into a building. At the firehouse, a proby's tasks might include checking radio batteries, filling canteens with water, mopping the floors, making coffee, etc. In a light vein, a proby is often expected to be a gopher at the bidding of senior colleagues.

**◆ Job Outlook**

**◆ The Ground Floor**

**On-the-Job Responsi-bilities**

◆ *Beginners or Experienced Firefighters*

❑ Respond to fire alarms and other emergency calls
❑ Connect hose lines to fire hydrants and to the pump engine
❑ Select the proper hose nozzle and direct water or chemicals onto the fire
❑ Climb ladders to reach upper levels of buildings
❑ Break windows and/or vent the roof to let smoke and heat out of the building
❑ Create openings in the building for firefighters' entrance
❑ Assist people out of burning structures
❑ Give first aid to victims of burns or smoke inhalation; administer CPR
❑ Communicate with superior during firefighting effort over a portable two-way radio
❑ After the fire is out, remain on the scene and do clean up
❑ Take up hundreds of feet of hose line

Between fire alarms, duties may include:
❑ Check and maintain fire hydrants in the fire station's area
❑ Inspect boilers and oil burners in area buildings and check for other potential fire hazards
❑ Give talks on fire prevention and fire safety to school children, civic groups and others
❑ Check and maintain all equipment at the firehouse

**When You'll Work**

◆ Firefighting goes on 24 hours a day, which means shiftwork. The workweek at municipal departments can vary greatly, from 40 to 56 hours, although the national average is 50.8 hours. No one watches a clock during a fire, so it's never quitting time until the fire is out.

Two of the most common shifts are the 24-hour tour and the split shift. In the first, the firefighter works 24 hours of duty, then gets either 48 or 72 hours off duty. In the split shift, firefighters typically work three or four days on a nine-hour dayshift (typically 9 A.M. to 6 P.M.); and three or four nights on a 15-hour tour ( 6 P.M. to 9 A.M.), then get three or four days off before repeating the cycle.

Vacation days vary. A small department may offer anywhere from six to ten vacation days to start, whereas a big department may be much more generous. In New York City, for example, even new hires get 20 days of vacation.

Major holidays are paid, and those who have to work on a holiday generally earn time-and-a-half. In some major departments, however, all firefighters are paid the same for holidays, whether they are on-duty or not.

◆ **Time Off**

❑ College tuition reimbursement for advanced studies in fire training
❑ Generous medical, dental and disability insurance
❑ Uniforms and safety equipment generally provided
❑ Option to retire at half-pay, typically at age 50 or after 20 to 25 years of service

◆ **Perks**

❑ Municipal fire departments (city, town or village governments)
❑ State or federal government agencies (e.g., Veterans Administration hospitals, Forest Service or Park Service)
❑ Private firefighting companies (e.g., to protect an oil refinery)
❑ Manufacturing companies (large and/or remote industrial plants may have their own fire service)

◆ **Who's Hiring**

**Entry-level or experienced firefighters:** little travel potential

Firefighters regularly attend training seminars in their local area. They also may attend yearly conventions at the state level, but not all fire departments pay travel expenses.

◆ **Places You'll Go**

**Surroundings**

Some fire stations, especially in expanding suburban communities, are sleek, modern, one-story structures with state-of-the-art equipment. Others are aging, paint-peeled buildings furnished with the firefighters' own hand-me-downs or donated items from the neighborhood.

Between alarms, firefighters have fire drills and training exercises. They check their equipment daily—a missing or malfunctioning part could threaten a firefighter's safety. Then there are routine housekeeping duties: cleaning the firehouse and preparing meals. Most career firehouses have sleeping and dining areas; volunteer companies may not.

**On-the-Job Hazards**

❑ Susceptibility to smoke inhalation, serious burns or injury from building collapse
❑ Exposure to many hazardous chemicals and materials
❑ Possible exposure to AIDS, hepatitis and other diseases (those who rescue bleeding fire or accident victims)
❑ Danger of personal harm when firefighting in hostile environments such as civil disturbances, where some people may try to hinder firefighters' efforts by damaging their equipment or attacking them

**Dollars and Cents**

Pay levels depend on the size of the department, the region and the person's experience. According to the 1992 edition of the *Municipal Year Book,* which surveys the salaries of public employees in more than 1,000 cities, the average starting salary for all firefighters was $22,237; the average maximum salary was $28,861 (for firefighters who have not been promoted to the next rank).

Not surprisingly, the biggest cities usually pay the highest salaries. In Chicago, a new hire could expect to earn $28,380 in 1991, whereas one in Columbus, Ohio, would make $17,992. In New York City, a firefighter starts at $29,500, and earns $42,773 after five years. Overall, starting salaries are highest in the West and lowest in the South.

Typically there is also extra pay for the night shift (''shift differential''); longevity pay after five or more years of service; and time-and-a-half for overtime. The great majority of career firefighters (190,000) belong to a union, the International Association of Fire Fighters, which helps negotiate their pay and benefits.

The annual edition of the *Municipal Year Book*, published by the International City Management Association, lists updated salaries of firefighters in several hundred U.S. cities. It can be usually found in public libraries.

You often must work three to five years or more before becoming eligible for promotion. In addition to how well you score on civil service exams, your job performance rating, seniority and additional training are factors in whether you will be promoted. Generally, the promotional path is to lieutenant, then captain, battalion chief, deputy chief, and, finally, chief. Many departments require a lieutenant to have an associate degree, and, increasingly, a captain to earn a bachelor's degree.

◆ **Moving Up**

Some firefighters who decide to leave the "action" become fire inspectors, working to prevent fires by enforcing fire safety laws in buildings. Others may leave the department altogether to become fire science specialists for private employers such as insurance companies, inspecting buildings to help set insurance rates or investigate arson. Many firefighters, however, are content to remain on the engine or truck for their entire careers.

Generally, large metropolitan areas have an all-career fire service, while small towns and rural areas are served by all-volunteer crews. As with the police force, New York City also can boast the biggest fire department—10,600 uniformed personnel. Other major departments include Los Angeles, Chicago, Philadelphia, Detroit, Phoenix, St. Louis and Atlanta. Some suburban communities may employ a handful of paid firefighters supplemented by many more volunteers.

◆ **Where the Jobs Are**

## Training

Many community and junior colleges have two-year programs in fire science and technology. (They do not, of course, replace the fire academy training.) Contact a local school for a catalog, or speak with a school guidance counselor.

Several publications are available to help tutor people who want to take the firefighters' civil service exams. These manuals give typical written questions and physical test procedures and often are available in libraries or in the careers section of bookstores. Titles include Arco's *Firefighter Civil Service Test Tutor,* by Robert Andriuolo and Barron's *How to Prepare for the Fire Fighter Examinations,* by James J. Murtagh.

## Making Your Decision: What to Consider

**The Bad News**

❏ Threat of injury or loss of life in daily work
❏ Having to work in all kinds of weather and on holidays
❏ Rotating shifts and changing sleep schedule are hard on the body
❏ Shift can be slow and boring, especially 24-hour tours
❏ Leaving a warm bed at 3 A.M. to go fight a fire
❏ Seeing the pain and injuries of others can be upsetting

**The Good News**

❏ Every day is different; no two runs are alike
❏ Work schedule permits lots of free time and flexibility
❏ Excitement of being at the center of the action
❏ Satisfaction of helping people and saving lives
❏ Instant results for your efforts
❏ Strong bonds, camaraderie with colleagues

Firefighting remains an overwhelmingly male profession: only 1.4 percent of career firefighters are women, according to the federal government. Typically the greatest obstacle female candidates face is passing the entrance tests for physical ability.

◆ **The Male/Female Equation**

Talking to the firefighters at the nearest station is a good place to start. They can tell you how to apply to take the next scheduled entrance exam (which may be given only once every year or two). Details about civil service exams can also be obtained from the city or state's Civil Service Commission (often listed in the telephone directory's "Blue Pages" of government offices). In big cities there may be a central personnel office or recruitment unit that will provide a brochure about the department.

◆ **More Information Please**

A career brochure on the fire service is available by writing:

National Fire Protection Association
Public Fire Protection Department
1 Batterymarch Park
P.O. Box 9101
Quincy, Massachusetts 02269-9101

A brochure about the career is available from the organization for both career and volunteer women in the field:

Women in the Fire Service
P.O. Box 5546
Madison, Wisconsin 53705
608-233-4768

You can get a bit of the flavor of "the life" from a publication targeted to firefighters:

*Firehouse*
PTN Publishing Co.
445 Broad Hollow Road
Melville, New York 11747
516-845-2700

# WHAT IT'S REALLY LIKE

**Kevin O'Hagan,** 25,
firefighter,
New York City Fire Department,
Engine Company 92, South Bronx, New York
Years in the job: 2½

**Why did you decide to become a firefighter?**
I'd been a (New York City) policeman for three years, since
I was 20. I liked the job, but I'd always wanted to be a fireman. My father was a two-star (fire) chief, my uncle was a
lieutenant and one of my brothers and three of my cousins
are firemen. So I decided to take the test for the fire department, and I did well on it.

**What was most difficult about your first fire?**
I was scared. My first day being a fireman was a thousand
times scarier than my first day as a cop. We had a working
fire in an apartment building. People don't realize a fire is
really hairy, and the way it spreads so fast is unbelievable.

They teach you everything in school but once the s—- hits
the fan, you forget it; you run around like a maniac. Luckily where I work all the guys are pretty seasoned; they take
you under their wing and they show you, which is great. In

32

my firehouse we have a pumper, a ladder truck with a tower ladder and a battalion chief. We get about one bad fire a day.

**How long was it before you felt confident in your skills?**
I guess about a year. In an engine company the whole crew works as one team. At the beginning of each tour we have a roll call and we're each given our assignment by the officer. The nozzle man puts the fire out; another guy backs him up because of the (water) pressure. The third guy is in charge of making sure they have enough hose to get upstairs and there are no kinks in it. The fourth guy is the driver; he's also in charge of the pumps and has to get water.

In the truck (ladder company) there are different positions. There are the guys that go inside, and there's an outside team. The senior guys get the tougher positions. The ladder company's job is to find the fire and tell you (the engine company) where it is, and to search for victims. A lot of times the doors are locked (in the building on fire) so they have all the tools to force the doors open.

**What do you do at the firehouse between fires?**
We have drill every day, and a lot of time we spend cleaning the tools. Usually the junior guy's job is to do most of the work. He cleans all the tools, cleans the firehouse, mops the floors.

**What do you like most about the work?**
You make a lot of friends in this job. I feel I'll have these friends for life—I can depend on them for anything. Also, the pay is pretty good; I never went to college. And the benefits are good—full medical, full dental, a prescription plan through the union.

**What do you like least about the work?**
The shifts, I guess. You have to work weekends sometimes, you're away from your family and you miss a lot of stuff because of that. We do two nine-hour day tours in a row, starting at 9 A.M. and working to 6 P.M. We're off two days, then we come in for two night tours that are 15 hours straight—from 6 P.M. to 9 A.M. Night tour is tough. When you come home from that first night you're shot, especially where I am because we're running out about 20 times a

tour. There are a lot of false alarms with the school kids.

Also, the public thinks we just sit around the kitchen all day and play cards and sleep all night, and that bugs me because I could get killed any time. I don't get any sleep at night when it's busy. Sometimes it seems like we're not appreciated.

**Have you ever been hurt on the job?**
I've been burned a few times . . . nothing serious, knock on wood. I've had sprains, but I haven't broken anything. I burned my ears and my neck. I was protected, but it's unbelievable how hot it can get. A lot of times it's so hot that you have to stay literally on the floor, on your stomach, and once you put water on the fire the steam is what burns you. Some people think our uniforms are fireproof but they're not. They protect you to a certain degree, but if it gets hot enough they can burn.

We're in a transition stage with our clothing. Our union is trying to get us ''bunker'' gear—it's like the space suit stuff. Bunker pants are the most important because I'd say most of our injuries are burns to the knees and legs.

**What would you say you're most proud of so far?**
I guess coming home alive every day.

**What advice would you give someone who's thinking about a firefighting career?**
It's a good job. But be aware that there's going to be a lot of things you see; you do see people get burned and it's kind of gory. You see dead people. We don't just go to fires, we go to heart attacks and car accidents, too. I've seen people decapitated in car accidents. You have to have a strong stomach. But like anything else, you get used to it.

## Karl Weber, 37,
### lieutenant, Elyria Fire Department,
### Elyria, Ohio
### Years in the job: seven

**How did you decide to become a firefighter?**
I'd worked in a factory for 12 years. They started making a

lot of changes that weren't for the benefit of the employees, so I decided it was time to get out. I wanted something service oriented, so when the tests came up for the police and fire department, I took them both. They only test here every two years. I passed, and from the time I took the initial test until I got hired it was about a year.

When I hired on we didn't go to fire school right away. We were put on shift, mainly as observers. My second night we had a rip-roaring house fire and were out from midnight until the next morning. I remember thinking, just what did I get myself into? After that, every time the alarm rang I expected another one of those. It really was the exception and not the norm, but since it was my first fire it opened my eyes. But by then I didn't have a choice—I'd already quit my other job!

**What was the most difficult part of the job at the start?**
Getting used to the lack of visibility during a fire. It's so dark from the smoke it's like you have blinders on. As you get close you begin to see where the fire is; you see it glowing or hear it popping and then go toward the sound.

That's why a movie like *Backdraft* is so unrealistic—there's never that kind of visibility. And that scene where that guy (actor Kurt Russell's character) is running into a building that's fully involved, with no air pack on, his coat open, his boots down, was ridiculous. We don't go anywhere without an air pack—not even a car fire. That's our standard operating procedure. We also wear a hood that covers our ears.

At first, it also was tough adjusting to being on the job for 24 hours at a time. I was used to working 7 A.M.to 3 P.M., then going home—not having another 17 hours ahead of me. We work 24-on, 24-off for three working days, then we're off for four days.

**How long did it take before you felt competent?**
It took a few years before I really felt I knew what I was doing. But even then, on the way to a fire you're still going over in your mind what you want to do first; what you're looking for. I don't think you ever get over that. In our department we don't get that many really big fires. We

get all kinds of car fires and garage fires and smoking barbecues.

**What's been your proudest achievement so far?**
We had a rip-roaring house fire one time about two in the morning. It was totally involved, and another guy and I went in and knocked it down in about two minutes. There was a victim inside and we got her out. A quick knockdown is what they teach you, and in this case everything went according to the book, which is unusual. It made us feel good to go in and do the job.

**You're on medical leave right now. How did you get hurt?**
We had a fire above the ceiling in an attic area. It was a suspended ceiling, and there was chicken wire nailed to the bottom of the trusses to keep the insulation from falling down to the ceiling. The insulation was on fire, so we were pulling all that stuff down. It was a real bear, and I just pulled too hard and felt something go in my shoulder. It turned out to be a rotator cuff injury and I eventually had surgery. I've been out about three months and am about to return to work.

**What routines do you have in your day?**
Typically you come in to the station at 8 A.M., go over the trucks, make sure everything's there, everything's working. We put in a couple hours of training around the station every day—just pulling equipment off the truck and using it. If you don't use it, you lose it. Sometimes we have instructors in from other departments for hazmat (hazardous materials) training and other things. We also do station maintenance—do the housework, make the beds, clean the toilets. But now that I'm a lieutenant I don't have to clean toilets anymore.

**What do you like most about your job?**
The flexibility of the time off. If I work Monday-Wednesday-Friday, I'm off Saturday through Tuesday.

**What do you like least about the job?**
Being in the public sector you can meet some wacky individuals, and they can be a pain sometimes. People call the fire department for stupid reasons. And at the fire scene

some people get in the way, driving over the hoses. I've almost been run over a couple times by drivers gawking at the fire as I'm trying to get equipment off the truck.

**Do you think much about the risks of your job?**
Not really. You try to be as careful as you can. Sometimes you have to take risks, but there's a difference between a calculated risk and an unnecessary risk. You try to calculate the odds and pick the safest route.

# Glenda Bonnett-Hopkins, 39,
## lieutenant, public education officer,
## Jacksonville Fire and Rescue Department,
## Jacksonville, Florida
## Years in the job: 13

**How did you get interested in the fire service?**
When I was eight years old, my sister's three-week-old baby died in a house fire. I remember thinking then that when I grew up, I would be a "fireman," and I would make sure nobody ever died in a fire. Of course, everybody would tell me, "Girls can't do that."

In 1979, I was working for the city as a clerk-typist. They put out a bulletin encouraging women to apply to the fire department, and I did. You took the written exam, and if you passed it, they brought you in for an oral interview. If you made it past that, you went in for the physical entry test.

**What was the test like?**
Very hard. I'm 5 feet, 6 inches tall, I weighed 140 pounds and I'd always been athletic. But when I learned there would be a 150-pound carry, I thought it would help me if I gained weight. I started working out, running up stairs and bleachers. I gained about 15 pounds, and it did help me some.

But what I found out was that the job really doesn't require a lot of brute strength; what you have to do is develop your own technique. Once you can master the skill and get over the clumsiness, the rest is just common sense.

I was one of four women who were hired provisionally. That meant if we passed the class (academy training), they would put us on probation. They had never had women go through the academy before. I was the only woman who graduated that year, although another was later hired under a court order. I was assigned to an engine company.

**How was it being the only woman on the job?**
It was terrible. Nobody would talk to me or eat with me. It was lonesome. I don't think people knew how to accept me. The station had mostly older guys, set in their ways. I felt I really had to prove myself to them, so I gave 299 percent of myself all the time to prove I could do it. But it seemed the more I did, the less impressed they were.

If it weren't for my family and my two brothers . . . I don't know. A lot of days I thought, Why am I here? Why am I doing this to myself? But then I'd think, if I quit, I'll be doing what they want me to do.

I stuck with it, and I made my one-year probation. But it (the atmosphere) didn't get much better. It went from ice cold to cold to tepid.

**How long did you stay at that station?**
About two and a half years, then I finally transferred out. I went to a station that had younger firefighters. It was easier to work with them, though it still took me a while to adjust.

My new station was a ladder company. I loved the work. I thought, I can't believe I've been missing this—getting to chop down doors, break out windows, put up ladders, rescue people. I felt, this is what the fire department's all about. I loved every minute of it. I had some rescues, and that made me want to get into fire prevention, to prevent these things from happening in the first place.

**How did you move into fire prevention?**
After six years in active firefighting I wanted to make a change. So when the department allocated some new positions in fire prevention I pushed real hard to get in, and I finally did. I'd been taking fire courses for several years, and I'd been going to local and national conferences. Then I started taking fire science classes to learn more about the chemistry of fire.

I mainly did fire inspections for businesses. But every once in a while I'd go to a school and do a little fire safety program. I'd attend education conferences, pick up a prepackaged (fire safety) program and adapt it. I also took junior college classes on education, learning how to develop my own curriculum.

More people started to write and call asking for talks and demonstrations. The department first said that I could do safety programs half a day each week. Then it got to be two days, then three days and eventually it was five days. I've been doing public education full-time now for three years.

**What do you like most about your work?**
I have a chief who truly believes in public education, so he gives me a lot of freedom and flexibility to go out and build on the programs.

**What do you like least?**
Having to turn somebody down when they ask for a program. We only have two people doing this full-time. The callers can't believe it. They say, you've got a thousand people in that fire department and you can't send anybody?

**What are you most proud of in your career?**
Just the fact that I toughed it out. Sometimes I look back and say, I can't believe I actually made it. It's smoother now; there are 17 women in the department. I'm one of the adjunct instructors at the training academy, so I get a chance to work with most of the females that go through the academy.

**What advice would you give someone—male or female— who's considering a firefighting career?**
What I always tell them on the first day of academy: make sure this is what you want to do. Don't look at this as an easy way to get paid. You have to be sincere because people's lives depend on your being able to do the job.

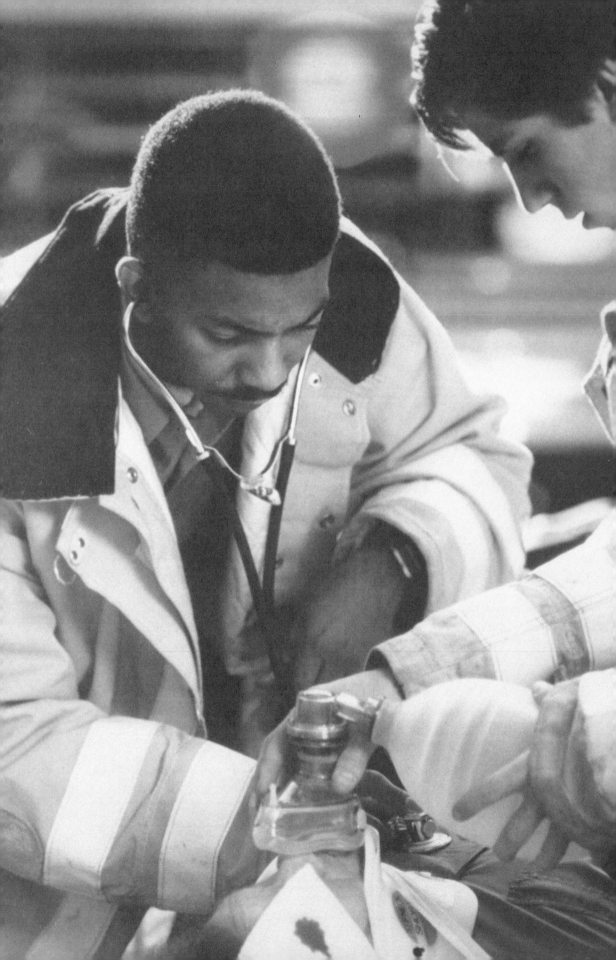

**With sirens wailing, the ambulance quickly heads for the scene of a medical emergency—a car accident, a heart attack, a choking child. The men and women inside the ambulance are called emergency medical technicians (EMTs). As the front line of the hospital medical team, it is their job to assess the victim's injury or illness and give expert help fast.**

At an emergency scene, EMTs may have to walk, climb or crawl over unsteady terrain and pull, push or lift victims to the ambulance. EMTs also may assist firefighters and other personnel in getting trapped victims out of a car wreck or collapsed structure.

No two ambulance runs are ever alike. Each situation is influenced by factors such as the nature of the call; the

41

severity of the illness or injury; the physical environment; even the personalities of the victims, their families and the responders themselves. The emergency scene may resemble organized chaos, and noise levels may be high, especially when many sirens are going at once.

Depending on whether they are trained to provide basic or advanced life support, EMTs do whatever they can for the victim while quickly heading for the nearest or most appropriate medical facility. The hood of the emergency vehicle often has the word "Ambulance" or "Rescue" spelled backwards so the motorists ahead can read it in their rearview mirrors—and pull over to give the ambulance the right-of-way.

Working in teams of two if not three, one EMT always remains in the rear of the ambulance with the patient. Keeping in radio contact with the dispatcher and/or the hospital, EMTs perform their duties according to strict training guidelines or under a doctor's step-by-step supervision. Most patient transport is done by ambulance, although some critically injured people may also be taken by helicopter or small plane to specialized trauma centers.

When the EMTs reach their destination, they inform the attending doctor or nurse of the patient's status and what care has been given. If they are not needed to assist in the emergency room with any further treatment, the EMTs head back to their home base to await the next call for help.

Of course, not every run involves a dramatic life or death situation. Most of the time, EMTs simply take care of people at many levels of need. On private services in particular, there may be a lot of basic transport work, for example, taking wheelchair-bound people from their homes to doctors' appointments, or transferring them from a hospital to a nursing home.

EMTs are never lonely. Especially on 24-hour shifts, they eat, wait and sleep with the other members of the squad at the home base. The nature of the job often creates a strong sense of camaraderie.

As one paramedic describes the work: "You never know what's around the next corner, and there's never a dull moment. You get self-gratification when you deliver a baby, bring back a cardiac arrest, or save someone from a major trauma. If you're an adrenaline junkie, this is the job for you."

## What You Need to Know

- ❏ Basic biology (how the body functions—the respiratory, circulatory, digestive and other systems)
- ❏ Basic anatomy (the structure and organs of the body)
- ❏ Basic physiology (the functions of the body's systems and organs)
- ❏ Medical terminology
- ❏ Use and care of basic emergency equipment, such as backboards and suction devices
- ❏ Patient handling and transport

## Necessary Skills

- ❏ First aid (emergency care for cuts, burns, choking, shock, bleeding)
- ❏ How to assess vital signs (blood pressure, pulse rate, body temperature)
- ❏ How to give CPR (cardiopulmonary resuscitation—a set of skills that can revive a person who has stopped breathing or whose heart has stopped)
- ❏ How to open a blocked airway (nose, mouth or upper throat) and give oxygen (ventilate)
- ❏ Verbal ability to clearly communicate with patients and doctors, in person and over radio equipment
- ❏ Good writing skills (to write reports of patient's treatment and other relevant information)
- ❏ Keen powers of observation to quickly assess a patient's condition
- ❏ Good driving skills; good sense of direction is helpful

## Do You Have What It Takes?

- ❏ Self-confidence to be able to take charge of a situation
- ❏ Common sense, good judgment
- ❏ Ability to stay calm and act quickly under stress
- ❏ Strong sense of responsibility
- ❏ Emotional stability, even temper
- ❏ Patience to deal with confused or difficult patients
- ❏ Ability to improvise; there are few "textbook" runs

◆ **Getting into the Field**

43

❏ Willingness to work shifts, holidays and weekends
❏ Ability to tolerate different conditions such as extreme heat, cold and wetness
❏ Have a ''strong stomach'' and not be squeamish at the sight of blood or serious injuries

## Physical Attributes

❏ Excellent health and in good physical condition
❏ Physical stamina, especially for 24-hour shifts
❏ Good vision (corrective lenses permitted). Accurate color vision is required both for safe driving and ability to see diagnostic signs such as blue lips.
❏ Finger dexterity to insert hypodermic needles into veins, tie tourniquets, wrap bandages, etc.
❏ Manual dexterity to give artificial respiration, operate equipment
❏ Strength and motor coordination for lifting and carrying victims onto stretchers and into an ambulance (physical tests generally require lifting and carrying up to 125 pounds, 250 pounds with assistance)
❏ Normal hearing (for tasks such as listening to a patient's breathing, communicating over radio)

## Education

A high school diploma or equivalency is generally required to begin EMT training. Applicants usually must be at least 18 years of age.

There are three training classifications of EMTs: basic, intermediate and paramedic. EMT-basic training usually consists of 110 classroom hours, plus clinical experience in a hospital emergency room and fieldwork observing professionals on an ambulance. EMT-intermediate training usually involves another 90 to 110 hours of coursework, while paramedic training averages about nine months of extensive study.

At every level after training is completed, students must take both a written exam and a ''practical,'' demonstrating their skills. A passing grade earns them a state certificate.

## *Licenses Required*

All states require certification of EMTs. Some states conduct their own certification program or allow the option of getting registration from the National Registry of Emergency Medical Technicians. Thirty states require national registration at some or all levels of certification. Registered EMTs use the initials NR, as in NREMT-P. All EMTs must be recertified (or reregistered), usually every two years.

All EMTs also must have a valid driver's license.

A note on terminology: various states may award EMTs a certificate, license or registration. Certification (or registration) is essentially the process of completing training requirements and demonstrating a level of competency; a license is the permit to work.

**Job openings will grow:** about as fast as average

Competition is most keen for positions in fire department squads, which pay the most. Private ambulance companies, which generally pay less, have more openings. Paramedics, who have the highest level of training, are in greatest demand.

### Job Outlook

**Entry-level job:** EMT-Basic (also called EMT-Ambulance or EMT-A)

Generally, if an EMT-Basic is paired with an EMT-Intermediate or Paramedic, the EMT-Basic will do the driving, so that the more advanced colleague can assist the patient in the back of the ambulance.

### The Ground Floor

The actual categorization of specific tasks varies from state to state. For example, some states train an EMT-Basic to do defibrillation (an electrical shock to "start up" a stopped heart); others teach it at the intermediate or even paramedic level.

EMT-Basics perform the following tasks:

❑ Restore patient's breathing and administer oxygen
❑ Apply bandages and splints

### On-the-Job Responsibilities

❏ Control bleeding
❏ Assist in emergency childbirth
❏ Monitor vital signs
❏ Give initial treatment for poison, burns or shock
❏ Immobilize fractures
❏ Remove or help remove injured people from the scene of an accident
❏ After a run replace used linens, replenish supply of drugs or oxygen, sterilize certain equipment, etc.
❏ At least once each shift, check the vehicle: oil, gas, water in battery and radiator, tire pressure

EMT-Intermediates (sometimes called EMT-Advanced) perform all of the above tasks plus:

❏ Assess trauma patients
❏ Give intravenous (IV) fluids to trauma patients
❏ Place antishock trousers on trauma victims to improve blood circulation
❏ Perform advanced airway management and ventilation techniques

EMT-Paramedics perform all of the above tasks plus:

❏ Give drugs orally or by injection (venipuncture)
❏ Operate advanced cardiac monitoring equipment
❏ Interpret results of an EKG (the heartbeat's electric currents monitored by an electrocardiograph machine)
❏ Insert endotracheal tube (cylinder passed down the throat into the windpipe to deliver oxygen)

## When You'll Work

Very generally, fire department and hospital-based ambulances tend to work in shifts of 24 hours on-duty and 48 hours off, which means they work only nine or ten days a month. Municipal "third service" ambulances and private ambulance companies are more likely to have shifts of 8 or 12 hours.

EMTs who work for private ambulance firms and hospitals tend to work a 40-hour week, while fire and police EMS employees may work up to 56 hours a week.

New hires generally get two weeks of vacation after a year of service. Some holidays are paid.

Generally speaking, summer is a very busy time for all emergency medical personnel. If several EMTs want to vacation during the same period, the most senior person is likely to get the nod.

◆ **Time Off**

Fringe benefits vary widely, depending on the region and the competition for recruits.

❏ Medical, dental and life insurance
❏ Liability insurance (e.g., you may be named in a civil suit by patients who claim your medical treatment was inappropriate or inadequate)
❏ Paid vacation and sick leave
❏ Tuition reimbursement for EMS courses
❏ Paid attendance for seminars and conferences
❏ Uniforms or clothing allowance provided
❏ Retirement and pension plans

◆ **Perks**

❏ Police and fire department ambulance squads
❏ Hospital-based ambulance services
❏ City or county emergency services departments
❏ Private ambulance services
❏ Industrial and manufacturing plants (for in-house EMS, especially where chemicals and hazardous materials are used)
❏ Military bases (some contract for civilian EMS coverage)
❏ Health agencies
❏ Community colleges and hospitals (for EMT instructors)
❏ Ski patrols, resorts
❏ Park services

◆ **Who's Hiring**

EMTs who work for police department emergency medical units are also sworn police officers. EMTs who work for fire departments generally are cross trained as firefighters.

**On-the-Job Hazards**

❏ Potential for traffic accident while responding to a call (not all automobile drivers hear ambulance sirens or see their lights, or give the ambulance the right-of-way)

❏ Back injuries from heavy lifting of equipment and injured people

❏ Exposure to infectious blood, body fluids, airborne viruses and other diseases

❏ Potential exposure to chemicals and hazardous materials sometimes found at a fire or an explosion

❏ Smoke inhalation, exposure to extreme heat at scene of fire

❏ Threat of electrocution if there are downed electrical wires at accident site

❏ Potential for injury in unsafe or collapsed structures

❏ Possible violence from disturbed or combative patients

**Places You'll Go**

**All EMT levels:** some travel potential

Because of the constant need to stay on top of medical developments and qualify for recertification, EMTs frequently attend training seminars that may be paid for by their employer. Some of these may be out of town.

**Surroundings**

When they're on call, EMTs spend much time outdoors in all types of weather and in various environments. At their home base, they may be able to relax between calls. Squads that work 24-hour shifts generally provide sleeping quarters. There may not always be cooking facilities, but there usually is at least a table at which to sit and eat.

**Dollars and Cents**

Pay varies enormously, depending on the region, the type of employer, the person's level of training and the length of service. Of all EMS providers, fire departments pay the highest salaries. Overall, the West pays the best in all job categories, while the Southeast pays the least. Generally, overtime is paid on a time-and-a-half basis.

According to the 1992 Journal of Emergency Medical Services (JEMS) Salary Survey, which monitors salary trends among some EMS providers around the country, the average starting and maximum salaries for the three levels were:
EMT-Basics: $19,213–$31,249
EMT-Intermediates: $19,940–$26,076
Paramedics: $24,621–$33,059

As EMTs progress to each training level, they take on greater responsibility and earn more money. Earning national registration may also make higher-paying jobs easier to get.

**◆ Moving Up**

Because the paramedic level is the top rank, further advancement generally means leaving direct patient care. A paramedic might become a supervisor or director of the ambulance corps. Some go into emergency medical services administration at the city, county or state level. Candidates for such promotions need to show a strong base of knowledge in the field and leadership abilities, and increasingly are being required to have a bachelor's degree in EMS or a related field such as nursing or public health administration.

Some EMTs who work for a fire department squad switch into full-time firefighting. Some transfer to the other end of the two-way radio and become emergency dispatchers. Others may choose to remain in health care by returning to school to become registered nurses or even doctors. Finally, some move into sales or marketing of emergency medical equipment.

The majority of the nation's estimated 575,000 licensed EMS personnel are volunteers, and most of them are EMT-basics. Approximately 89,000 EMTs have paid positions, and most of them are paramedics. A little more than one third of paid personnel work for private providers; one third work for municipal police, fire or rescue squad departments; and one quarter work for hospitals.

Paid positions are concentrated in large metropolitan

**◆ Where the Jobs Are**

areas. Small towns and rural communities typically are served by all-volunteer squads.

**Training**

It's fairly easy to find EMT training. EMT-basic and intermediate courses may be offered by municipal police, fire and health departments; hospitals and ambulance services; and on a nondegree basis by community and junior colleges. Basic and intermediate classes typically meet for two or three hours twice weekly over four months and may cost little or a few hundred dollars. Paramedic training typically lasts about nine months, is not as widely available and may cost up to $1,000.

Specific certification requirements for all levels are available from the state's Director of Emergency Medical Services. That department usually is listed in the ''state government'' section of the telephone directory.

States that do not conduct their own EMT certification procedure accept registration from the National Registry of Emergency Medical Technicians. If you have current national registration and you move to another state, generally you do not have to be certified again in the new state.

A candidate for national registration must have completed the appropriate coursework for each level, and pass both written and practical exams. Information about the registration process is available from:

National Registry of Emergency Medical Technicians
6610 Busch Boulevard
P.O. Box 29233
Columbus, Ohio 43229
614-888-4484

**The Male/Female Equation**

Most emergency medical technicians are male. In the 1992 JEMS Salary Survey of EMS providers, women accounted for 5 percent of the EMT-Basics, 7 percent of EMT-Intermediates, and 15 percent of Paramedics. Hospitals, private ambulance services and nonprofit services employ the highest percentages of women. Their numbers are lowest in cross-trained fire departments.

**The Bad News**

❏ Long shifts, stressful situations
❏ Work is physically demanding
❏ Work involves tragedy and can be emotionally draining, causing burnout
❏ Risk of exposure to infectious diseases
❏ Potential for lawsuits from patients treated

**The Good News**

❏ Satisfaction of helping people, seeing the results of your care
❏ Constant challenge
❏ Respect from the public, being treated as a professional
❏ Not being tied to a desk eight hours a day
❏ Flexibility of having several days off at a time

◆ **Making Your Decision: What to Consider**

Good places to start include the local ambulance corps, hospitals, police and fire departments and health departments. Ask a local community college for its catalog, or speak with a high school guidance counselor.

A list of state EMS directors and paramedic training sites also is available from:

National Association of Emergency
Medical Technicians
9140 Ward Parkway
Kansas City, Missouri 64114
816-444-3500

◆ **More Information Please**

Reading a publication for EMS personnel can help give you a sense of the job. Jems Communications publishes *Journal of Emergency Medical Services* and *Rescue* magazines. For information and/or reprints of the complete 1992 JEMS Salary Survey, contact:

Emergency Care Information Center
Jems Communications
1947 Camino Vida Roble, Suite 200
Carlsbad, California 92008
619-431-9797

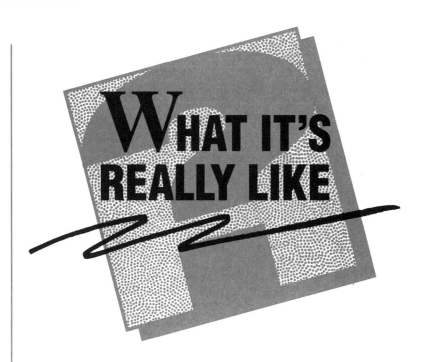

# WHAT IT'S REALLY LIKE

**Mary Boston, 31,**
paramedic, Lakewood Hospital
Emergency Medical Service,
Lakewood, Ohio
Years in the field: ten

**How did you get involved in emergency health care?**
I always wanted to be in the medical field, so years ago I
got my EMT-Basic training at a community college. A lot
of EMTs start out in the private ambulance business, but I
didn't really want to do that because I'd rather have more
action. Back then, EMTs were mostly on private squads
where they just did hospital-to-hospital or hospital-to-
nursing home transport.

I figured the best way to get a foot in the door of Cleveland's department of emergency medical services (EMS)
would be to start dispatching for them (a private company
handled the dispatch). You had to have an EMT certificate
to be an EMS dispatcher. They had an opening, and I got
the job.

**What was the work like?**
Busy. We often got up to 100 calls on an eight-hour shift. I

became really interested in all of the calls; I was curious about what was going on at the other end of the phone. I dispatched for about a year and a half, then I applied to the EMS department and I was hired.

**So now you were at the other end of the phone. What was the hardest part of the job at first?**
Dealing with a lot of different people—all kinds of races, age groups, sicknesses. It was overwhelming at first. I liked the action, but I was wondering all the time if I was doing everything right.

I started out as a "third person," going around observing two other trained paramedics. Then I became a team with one other person.

**How long was it before you felt confident in your skills?**
Not long; about three or four months. Working for a big city, I got more experience because of the numerous runs—about 12 runs in an eight-hour shift. When you're constantly getting calls, you get used to seeing the seizure or the cardiac arrest or the asthma attack. I was able to handle trauma; it's a big difference when you have so much trauma. Now I'm at Lakewood where it's smaller, and they may see only one or two traumas a year.

I worked for Cleveland for two years. While I was working I went to class and got my paramedic degree. Being a paramedic is a lot more satisfying because you're allowed to do a lot more.

**Is there any difference in the work on a hospital-based ambulance?**
It seemed like a vacation—I was going on about half as many runs as before. Also, we had to work certain hours in the emergency room, which is unusual. We would start IVs and draw blood, so I had opportunities to improve even more on my skills.

Another plus is that here a police officer responds to every one of our calls. It's a great help because they all know CPR, and they'll do it for us while we're starting IVs. They know where our equipment is in the truck, and they get it for us. We're on the same (radio) frequency as the police department, and a lot of times the police officer beats us to the call. In Cleveland we sometimes got on shooting scenes before the cops did.

**How do you feel about working 24-hour shifts now?**
Great. I only work nine days a month. You have so much time off, you can have a part-time job, you can go to school, you can do a lot more things.

It is getting busier at night, so we try to split the night when we can. We have four people (two ambulances) on a shift, and the first two take runs from 10 P.M. till 3:30 in the morning while the others rest. The second group takes runs from 3:30 till 9 in the morning. We worked out this schedule ourselves.

**Is there a routine to such unpredictable work?**
First thing in the morning we check the log book to see if anything happened on the previous shift that we need to be aware of. We check the ambulances to take an inventory of equipment and supplies, restock the oxygen, get gas. We check the activity calendar, which shows any community activity we need to do such as teaching CPR to the Boy Scouts or to a business. We may be scheduled to attend a lecture or a continuing education activity, such as meeting with the fire department about extrication techniques.

**What do you like the most about the work?**
Helping others. I know it sounds corny and everybody says that, but I like it. It's just amazing to see a diabetic who's unconscious, and you give them sugar and they wake up—it's just very rewarding. Not that you're out there saving lives every day; most of the time you don't have situations that dramatic.

**What do you like the least?**
All the contagious diseases you can get. That's the scary part. You've got to be really cautious. We always wear gloves; we always have them in our pockets and in our coats.

**You've decided to become a registered nurse. Why?**
I want a good part-time job. It's not as easy to get part-time work as a paramedic. Nursing pays a lot, and I thought it would be an easy career for me because it's just a little

more in-depth than being a paramedic. I've got all of my prerequisites on account of having my associate degree—I worked that in while I was dispatching—so I don't have to take all the sciences over again. I started two years ago, and I'll be finished in May.

**What advice would you give someone who's thinking about a career as an EMT?**
You have to be able to deal with a lot of people. You have to think and act—you can't delay. Physically it can be challenging; there's a lot of lifting. And there are always new things to learn, there are always new methods coming up. Paramedics have to recertify in advanced cardiac life support every two years, and we have to have 70 hours of continuing education in that time.

In this job you're not rewarded a lot by people, and you're not often thanked, so it's got to come from within. And it does. I know for myself that it's rewarding.

### **Chris Marshall,** 22, NREMT-Intermediate, Metropolitan Emergency Medical Services (MEMS), Little Rock, Arkansas Years in the field: 2½

**How did you get into this field?**
I started out as a volunteer firefighter in the town where I lived. After high school, I went to EMT school hoping to become a firefighter some day. But when I rode the ambulance as part of my EMT training, I just fell in love with it. Helping others is one of the things I've always wanted to do.

I went to EMT-Basic school two nights a week for about four months. I got my certification and national registration, put in my application at MEMS and was hired. About three months later I started EMT-Intermediate training. I knew I wanted to be a paramedic one day so this was another step up the ladder.

**Who does what on an ambulance run?**
MEMS is a paramedic service, which means there's always
a paramedic on every unit. The paramedic has ultimate
control of the patient, but we're a team out there and we
work together. In our service, an intermediate can start IVs
for trauma only—say, someone who's been in a motor vehicle accident or a shooting—and there are a couple tubes
you can put in the airway. Those two things are the main
difference between a basic and an intermediate.

The paramedic always has to ride in the back (with the patient), so the other EMT has to drive. I've been doing all
the driving. Fifteen miles over the speed limit is all we're
allowed to go. If we're "running hot," we have to have our
lights and our siren on, and if we have the red light at an
intersection, we have to come to a complete stop and make
sure there's no traffic coming and that everybody sees us
and that they stop before we go on through. We don't just
run through the light.

I do want to ride in the back, though. That's why I went to
paramedic school. I went two nights a week for almost a
year. I just took my national registry exam. I'm waiting to
be certified, so I can't work yet as a paramedic.

**What was the hardest part of the job at the start?**
Being calm in an emergency situation. I can remember
when I was just shaking . . . I was scared because I was
new at it. My partner would tell me to take a deep breath
and relax and slow down—that if I was nervous it was going to be hard to help somebody else.

**Have there been situations where someone's life was
depending on you?**
Yes. Depending on me to get them to the hospital alive in a
safe and timely manner. That's happened several times.

**What's a typical day like?**
We work a 12-hour shift, 6:30 A.M. to 6:30 P.M. I work two
days, then I'm off two days. During the day we have 12
ambulances on duty, at night there are seven or eight.
We're all spread out. Our service has six stations, and if
we're not on call, they'll send us to one of the stations and
we'll just sit and watch TV and relax.

The days equal themselves out. Some days are really, really busy, and other days we might have only four or five runs. It makes the day go by faster when you're busier and you get to see more people.

**What do you like most about the work?**
I like the atmosphere, the people I work with. It's like another family to me more than anything. When you're out on your ambulance, you're more or less your own boss. You have protocols you have to follow as far as patient care goes, but when you're not with a patient you can pretty much do what you want.

**What do you like least about the work?**
There's a lot of stress, that's the down thing.

**What advice do you have for someone thinking about this career?**
Have dedication to the work and a willingness to learn. You're always learning something new. If your local ambulance service allows people who aren't EMTs to ride along, that would be a good thing because you kind of get a feel for it. Some people hear the siren, and that really gets their adrenaline going, but you have to realize the job is a lot more than that.

## Earl Forsythe, 30,
"Angel 3" helicopter flight paramedic, STAT (Specialized Treatment and Transport) Pittsburgh, Pennsylvania Years in the field: nine

**What is the STAT service?**
It's a consortium of seven hospitals, providing air and ground medical transport. We have one critical care ground transport unit in addition to three helicopters—Angel 1, 2, and 3—and one airplane.

**How did you get involved in this career?**
At age 14 I was a junior member of the local volunteer fire department, which basically meant I was just allowed to

hang around. When I was older the department sent me for my EMT-Basic training.

I started college to get a business degree, then I transferred to mortuary school with plans to become a funeral director. But after my first year I decided to postpone college for a year to work and make some extra money in another field. One year stretched to several; eventually the recession hit and I was laid off. All I had to fall back on was having been a volunteer EMT. I knew there were ambulance services willing to pay me, so it was something I could step into quickly. In 1984, I was hired by an ambulance service that in turn sent me for my paramedic training.

**How many jobs have you had in the field?**
Three before STAT. Each time I moved for fewer hours and more pay. I went from a municipal authority ambulance service to a private, nonprofit organization, to a private ambulance service, then here. I've been with STAT three and a half years.

**Are all your helicopter patients in critical condition?**
Probably 75 percent of the patients, although critical, are stable enough that we're not working our butts off on them. It's the other 25 percent we work on furiously to keep alive during the flight to the hospital.

Each crew is made up of a paramedic and a nurse, and the pilot. We have to do things very quickly, especially if we're dealing with trauma patients. I'm sure you've heard of the "golden hour" (a trauma patient's chances of dying increase 1 percent every minute they have to wait for medical care), and sometimes so much of that golden hour has been used up by the time we get to the patient.

**What's a typical day like for you?**
We have a daylight shift (7:30 A.M. to 7:30 P.M.) and a midnight shift (the reverse). We rotate every week. On daylight, we do follow-ups on any patients that we've flown in in the last 48 hours. You call wherever that patient is and get a follow-up on their condition, usually from the nurse in charge. Then we call back the hospital or ambulance service that originally called us for that patient and give them an update.

We also have to make sure all the supplies on the helicopters are updated, that any battery-operated equipment is fully charged. In frigid weather, we make sure the helicopter stays warm so that none of the drugs freeze.

We can sleep on the midnight shift if there are no calls. We average between 150 and 200 flights a month among all three helicopters, and the flights are pretty evenly distributed. Most flights come during daylight or evening hours, so it's very rare when you're not able to sleep on the midnight shift.

**What do you like most about this work?**
A whole lot, actually. Certainly after starting in the trenches—in my first job I worked 60 hours a week for $10,000 a year—the working conditions here are great. We work 40 hours, and the pay is much better.

There also seems to be more of a camaraderie among the crew in air medicine. I think part of the reason for that is although you're always at risk for any type of accident, you stand a better chance of surviving an ambulance crash than a helicopter crash. I personally have been involved in a couple of situations that were very, very close. So in the back of our minds we always know there is a great risk in our job, and I think that pulls us all a little closer.

**What do you dislike about the work?**
That you can't save everybody. Some patients have greater impact on you than others, especially the pediatric patients. I've always had a problem (dealing emotionally) with the kids. But after I became a father, it really hit home because I'm able to see a little bit of my son in every kid we fly.

**What advice would you give to someone considering this career?**
Really consider why you're getting into it. You're not going to get rich, it's not an easy way to make a living. I've seen so many people jump into it and be gone in two years, if that, because it just wasn't what they thought it'd be. So "road test" it if you can. There are many volunteer corps around the country, and they're so short on help they'd welcome you.

**A terrified six-year-old dials 911 and cries, "My mommy's on the floor and I can't wake her up!" A distraught woman pleads, "My husband is having a heart attack—what should I do?" A frightened senior citizen alone at home whispers, "Someone is breaking into my house!" At a time of panic, each of them has reached for the telephone in search of help.**

At the other end of the line, a reassuring voice is ready to give that help—the voice of the radio dispatcher. Often he or she is the unsung hero of emergency services. Depending on their function, dispatchers may help catch criminals, put out fires, save lives or deliver babies in the course of a day's work.

Dispatchers get the details fast: the caller's location, the problem, the severity. They quickly decide what units should respond—a police patrol car, a fire truck, an ambulance or all three—and send them to the scene of the emergency. In a medical crisis, a trained dispatcher will stay on the line with the caller until the ambulance gets there, giving "pre-arrival instructions" such as how to perform cardiopulmonary resuscitation (CPR).

These cool heads are generally called public safety dispatchers or telecommunicators. They work for police and fire departments, emergency medical services departments (EMS) or centralized communications centers that handle all emergency calls for a city or county.

In many cities, the police department is the nerve center, and all 911 calls come to the police dispatcher. Calls that do not involve the police are then transferred to the appropriate fire or ambulance service. In the many communities that do not yet have a 911 system, callers dial whatever emergency seven-digit telephone number has been designated for the police or fire departments. Many dispatch departments prioritize their calls, which means life-threatening situations get attention first. Not every call is an emergency—even if the caller thinks so—and it is the dispatcher's job to decide.

In some departments, dispatchers manually write all relevant information from a caller onto a complaint card. Larger or newly modernized departments usually have some type of computer-aided dispatch (CAD) system. The CAD dispatcher types information from the caller into a computer so that it is displayed on a monitor.

You must be at least 18 years old, have no criminal record and usually must pass a written civil service exam to qualify for a job as a dispatcher. Sometimes these exams are given very infrequently, perhaps only once every two or three years, so you may be hired on the condition that you pass the next scheduled test.

A dispatcher truly is connected to the community and the needs of its people. But the job pace is fast and the pressure high. You may have to work nonstop with only short breaks, taking one call after another. You may have to talk on the radio and the telephone at the same time. You'll need nerves of steel and plenty of patience. But your daily reward will be knowing that your efforts, and those of the workers you dispatch, can make the difference in saving someone's life.

*What You Need to Know*

❑ Basics of radio broadcasting
❑ Government (FCC) broadcast rules and procedures (e.g., swearing is not allowed on the radio)
❑ Operating procedures for 911 systems
❑ Radio broadcast techniques, which may include the numerical codes used by some police agencies (for quick routine messages such as "10-4," meaning "affirmative")
❑ The geographical area served by the department
❑ Telephone techniques; how to gather information from callers
❑ Crime terms and definitions (e.g., to tell police whether they're responding to an armed robbery in progress or a burglary that's already occurred)
❑ Fire and medical terms (e.g., to know what types of apparatus to send to a fire; how to accurately describe an ambulance patient's condition)

*Necessary Skills*

❑ How to operate a radio console
❑ How to operate a teletype machine
❑ How to operate a computer-aided dispatch system (if in use)
❑ How to instruct a caller to give first aid and CPR (a set of skills that can revive a person who has stopped breathing or whose heart has stopped) until the ambulance arrives
❑ Typing skill usually necessary, computer familiarity helpful
❑ Experience on a telephone switchboard helpful
❑ Good oral communication skills, clear diction
❑ Good note taking for maintaining records and preparing written reports
❑ Ability to read maps

## Do You Have What It Takes?

- ❏ Ability to follow spoken and written instructions
- ❏ Ability to make decisions under pressure
- ❏ Strong sense of responsibility
- ❏ Close attention to detail, good memory
- ❏ Even temperament, steady nerves
- ❏ Versatility to handle two or more tasks at once (a dispatcher may have to conduct radio and telephone conversations at the same time)
- ❏ Tact and patience to deal with the public, especially callers who may be hysterical or rude
- ❏ Ability to get along with others in close quarters
- ❏ Reliability, punctuality
- ❏ Willingness to work night and weekend shifts

### Physical Attributes

- ❏ Excellent hearing
- ❏ Stamina for sitting eight hours or more each shift
- ❏ Coordination and dexterity for operating electronic equipment and a radio console

### Education

High school diploma generally required. Helpful subjects include English, speech, psychology, electronics, social science and civics. Knowledge of a foreign language is a plus, as is first aid or other medical training.

### Licenses Required

None. In some states dispatchers need to be certified to operate a teletype or computer terminal linked to the state's Police Information Network or federal National Crime Information Center. A few states have a general certification training course for dispatchers, but it may not be mandatory.

## Job Outlook

**Job openings will grow:** about as fast as average
Since most public safety dispatchers work for state or local government, the number of job openings is affected

by municipal budget limitations or hiring freezes. Some agencies are converting from having sworn police personnel as dispatchers to hiring civilians, which will create more employment opportunities for those outside the police force. Many fire agencies look for ex-firefighters or current volunteer firefighters when screening dispatch applicants.

Generally, most openings will come from the need to replace dispatchers who leave the field. Turnover is relatively high because of work stress.

**Entry-level job:** dispatcher

Though all dispatchers generally perform the same duties, a new hire is likely to do more call taking (see below) until they become skilled at getting accurate information fast.

◆ **The Ground Floor**

A dispatcher's job involves two primary functions: call taking and dispatching. The call taker (also called complaint taker) is the one who first answers incoming calls; the dispatcher follows up and sets the needed response in motion. Usually the two work as a team. The success of the call depends on the skill and thoroughness of the call taker, who gets all the relevant information from the caller, types it into the computer (or writes it on complaint cards) and sends the message via computer screen or hands the card to the appropriate dispatcher. In small or low-volume departments there may be only one dispatcher on duty, and that person performs both functions.

◆ **On-the-Job Responsibilities**

Specific duties depend on the employer and type of service being provided. For example, police dispatchers use a teletype machine to quickly access state records when a police officer needs a check on a vehicle license plate (to see if the car has been reported stolen) or the driver's license (to see if the driver may be wanted on an outstanding warrant). A fire department dispatcher needs to understand different kinds of fires, the hazards they represent and the equipment that will be required to fight them. An EMS (emergency medical service) dispatcher typically knows at least CPR and first aid instruction. A dispatcher who works for a centralized communications department is likely to do it all.

### *Entry-level and Experienced Dispatchers*

❑ Receive all incoming calls on police and fire emergency numbers

❑ Take appropriate action, sending a patrol car, fire engines and/or ambulance as required

❑ Stay on line with caller as needed, serving as liaison between caller and responding units

❑ In EMS, give instructions to deal with choking, cardiac arrest, childbirth, etc. before ambulance arrives

❑ Run checks on driver's licenses, etc. over teletype and report back over police radio to patrol unit that made request

❑ Monitor burglar alarm systems and dispatch police as necessary

❑ Check on safety of police patrol units via scheduled call-ins

❑ Keep written log of calls or print out computer report of all calls at end of shift

## When You'll Work

Most public safety dispatchers work a 40-hour week. Since their services are needed around the clock, shiftwork is required, typically in eight-hour or 12-hour tours. Shifts usually are rotated on a weekly basis. Dispatchers may work a series of dayshifts, be off for two or three days, then return to work the nightshift for several nights. Some departments do offer a steady shift, where someone can work the dayshift or the nightshift all the time, although weekend work is still required.

## Time Off

Dispatchers usually earn at least a week's vacation after a year's service. Major holidays are paid. Those who work on a holiday are paid time-and-a-half or possibly double time.

Benefits vary widely, but may include:
❏ Medical and life insurance
❏ Liability insurance (e.g., dispatchers may be named in a civil suit by callers who claim that the dispatcher's medical instructions were wrong or the ambulance was not sent fast enough)
❏ Departments that require uniforms usually provide them or a uniform allowance
❏ Time off and paid expenses to attend training seminars
❏ Possible tuition reimbursement for job-related courses

◆ **Perks**

❏ Municipal police and fire/rescue departments
❏ County police or sheriff's departments
❏ State police and highway patrol departments
❏ Hospitals and private ambulance services
❏ County/regional communications centers
❏ State/county departments of emergency services

◆ **Who's Hiring**

**Beginners and experienced dispatchers:** little or no travel potential
You may attend an occasional local training seminar, but expenses may not be paid for an out-of-town professional convention.

◆ **Places You'll Go**

The ambience depends on the facility and its budget. Dispatchers may work in a modern, spacious, well-lighted, enclosed area with state-of-the-art equipment and functional furnishings. Others may work with aging equipment in windowless, cramped quarters where the noise level is high.
In any dispatch department there is virtually no privacy and almost no downtime, except perhaps in the wee hours of the nightshift. In very busy centers, dispatchers often eat meals at their stations, grabbing a bite between calls. And because the radio console area is shared among shift

◆ **Surroundings**

workers, there typically is no place for personal touches such as family photos or possessions other than a coffee mug.

**On-the-Job Hazards**

❑ Sitting all day may lead to low back strain
❑ Continual typing on computer keyboard (CAD units) may cause a repetitive stress nerve injury
❑ Soreness from hours of cradling telephone receiver between neck and shoulder (for those who don't have a headset)
❑ Constant stress and pressure may cause digestive or other medical problems

**Dollars and Cents**

There is a wide range of compensation for dispatchers, depending on the type of employer and the region. According to the 1992 Journal of Emergency Medical Services (JEMS) Salary Survey, fire departments pay dispatchers the most—an average of $31,135. Among all surveyed employers, the average starting salary was $20,032; the average top salary was $28,871. Salaries are highest in the central states and the West.

**Moving Up**

In most dispatch departments, the next step up means becoming a supervisor, which may involve training new employees. A front line supervisor generally still does some dispatching, whereas a manager or director no longer works the phones. Dispatchers at small departments may transfer to a large communications center, and some dispatchers move into the field for which they've dispatched—becoming police officers or firefighters. Those who have been trained as emergency medical technicians may go into direct patient care on an ambulance squad.

**Where the Jobs Are**

There were an estimated 70,000 jobs for public safety dispatchers in 1990. (Those who do not work in public safety include bus, train, truck and taxicab dispatchers, and gas and water service dispatchers.) The best job prospects are in urban areas and large communications centers.

Training requirements vary greatly, not only from state to state but from agency to agency within a state. According to the 1992 JEMS survey of more than 100 EMS systems around the country, about one third require dispatchers to have EMT training; another third require specialized dispatch training, and five percent require paramedic training. Thirty percent had no training requirements.

Generally, whether or not new hires get formalized classroom training, they typically will be observed by a more experienced dispatcher for several weeks before handling calls on their own. Others are sent to a course such as the 40-hour or 80-hour basic telecommunicator training program developed by the APCO Institute of the Associated Public Safety Communications Officers. The institute also offers a 32-hour Emergency Medical Dispatch (EMD) training and certification program, which has become the mandated EMD standard for various agencies in several states.

◆ **Training**

Figures for the industry as a whole are unavailable. But according to the 1992 JEMS survey, women make up 37 percent of EMS dispatchers. Most work in the public sector; the rest are primarily employed by private providers and hospitals.

◆ **The Male/Female Equation**

### The Bad News

❑ Stress and pressure due to the emergency nature of calls
❑ Being deskbound for 8 or 12 hours with few breaks
❑ Shiftwork, including weekends and holidays
❑ Possibility of being sued by a caller (claiming that your response was inappropriate or inadequate)

### The Good News

❑ Satisfaction of helping people in need
❑ A sense of self-worth and competence
❑ On some calls, knowing you made a difference
❑ Challenging work that's never boring

◆ **Making Your Decision: What to Consider**

## More Information Please

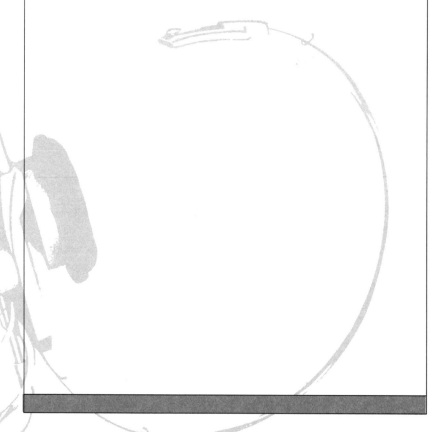

Start local: Ask your police or fire department or ambulance squad who provides their dispatching, and whom you might call for details. (Do NOT, of course, dial 911 for information!) As public safety dispatching generally is a civil service position, you could also contact your city or state Civil Service Commission for notification about the next scheduled exam.

Associated Public Safety Communications Officers, Inc. (APCO)
2040 S. Ridgewood Avenue
South Daytona, Florida 32119
904-322-2500

APCO is the oldest and largest professional membership organization of people in public safety communications. You can get general information about training or about a local chapter by contacting this organization.

**Debra Hair,** 31,
public safety dispatcher,
City of Yonkers Police Department,
Yonkers, New York
Years in the job: seven

**How did you get into this field?**
I'd been working in customer service and I didn't like the commute into Manhattan. A cousin of mine was doing dispatch, and I told her that her job sounded interesting. She sent me over to the city's civil service department to fill out an application. They hired me as a provisional employee until I could take and pass the test for public safety dispatch. The test is only given once every four years.

**What kind of training did you have?**
I was placed with other dispatchers who were like my twins. I sat with them at all times, for about two months. I listened in to see how they answered the calls, what questions they asked. If I picked up a phone they were listening to me. I also got some CPR training. In the last seven years things have changed very much. Now you get formal classroom training and a manual. The questions to ask callers are right in front of you.

71

**What services does your department dispatch?**
We do police, fire and ambulance. We don't have 911 yet, so all calls come in to the police via an emergency number or our regular nonemergency number. We receive about a million calls a year and do about 700,000 teletype entries. We have a staff of 29 dispatchers. On the day tour, we have six people on duty: two police call takers, two police dispatchers, one fire call taker and one fire dispatcher. The police dispatchers also handle the ambulance units.

**Which do you do?**
Everything. We rotate duties. If I'm a call taker, I get all the information from the caller, I enter it into CAD and transmit the job so it appears on everybody's screen. The appropriate dispatcher picks up the job and sees what it is. If she has a unit available, she sends it. If it's a priority (a life-threatening situation or other emergency) and she has to pull a car (off another call) she would then do so.

**What kind of hours do you work?**
We work eight-hour shifts. We used to rotate day/night shift every week, but now I'm on steady days. We're supposed to get 36 minutes for lunch, but if we took it we'd be leaving the burden for the other people. So basically we all just eat at the console and keep working.

**What was the hardest part of the job at the start?**
The stress factor is an unknown until you actually work it. I think at first I was overwhelmed—every time I picked up the phone I didn't know what was going to be there. I had to tell myself things like, "I can't fall apart because that cop on the street needs me right now. His life may be in my hands and I have to protect him."

**What kind of call is that serious?**
When a cop comes over the radio and tells you, "I'm in pursuit of a man with a gun," you say, "I want your location and a description." Then you air, "I have 301 car in pursuit of a male with a gun, subject is a white male wearing . . . " and you give a description, the location and which (other police) units are responding. You get them very quickly to tell you who's going for backup. You then have the air cleared again and call the first cop to update his location. You stay with it all the way.

**How long was it before you felt confident?**
It was a year before I felt, I've really got this, I can handle what I'm doing and I don't have to be nervous any more.

**What have been your proudest accomplishments?**
Probably good pursuits with radio cars. I remember a bank robbery that went down. I worked it with another dispatcher and between the two of us and the information we were getting on both channels, we did have an arrest. I pride myself on the fact that on most of the pursuits I get into, "my car" will get his person (suspect).

**What do you like most about the work?**
The variety. It's not mundane like typing letters every day. At any moment it could be totally calm, and the next minute all hell could break loose; your adrenaline pumps, the time just zooms by.

**What do you like least?**
Probably a bad call that can throw me for the day. When we find kids left unattended, sitting in dirty diapers, no food in the refrigerator—those kinds of things make me angry. When it comes to kids I still have a very soft spot.

But a call that would have upset me seven years ago usually doesn't today. Before, I would go home and think about it for hours: My God, that person died, what is his family thinking? I finally realized I couldn't keep bringing the job home because I could get five or ten calls a day like that. You have to learn to let it go.

Also, some callers can be rude and obnoxious, and they don't always tell the truth. For instance, most store owners have alarm systems. Many times they'll be involved in a dispute with a customer and they'll hit their holdup alarm button. The alarm company calls you up. You send police cars with lights and sirens believing there's a holdup—they get there and find that it is a dispute over 50 cents.

**What advice would you give someone considering this career?**
It definitely can be a very, very interesting job. But you have to have something of a lead stomach and nerves of steel. You have to condition yourself to the stress. If you're

at all wishy-washy or would faint at hearing words like, "She's bleeding from the mouth," it wouldn't be a job for you.

## Jeffrey McVey, 31, telecommunicator, Orange County Emergency Management, Hillsborough, North Carolina Years in the job: ten

**How did you get into this field?**
I'd gone to college for two years studying criminal justice, but I missed getting my associate degree by 40 hours or so. My family moved from Virginia to Wilmington, North Carolina before I finished.

I applied to be a police officer in the city of Wilmington. Several weeks went by, and then I got a call from an administrator in the police chief's office. They said the date was closed for police officer applications, but a telecommunicator's position was opening up in the police and fire department, if I'd be interested in that.

I was interviewed by three people for about 45 minutes. They had me talk into a recorder and they listened to my tone of voice, how clearly I spoke, how well I pronounced my words. After three weeks or so I got called in for a short interview. After another week the chief's office called and said I was hired.

**What sort of preparation did you have?**
It was on-the-job training. There was no manual, no classroom work, no book work at all before going on the radio console. When you look at a radio console with all those buttons and dials it's very intimidating, it looks like the console of an airplane.

For about two weeks I sat beside someone who was experienced; I put on a headset and just listened. Then they said, "Tonight's your night—we'll let you talk 30 minutes on the radio and give out a couple of calls. Just ease your way into this thing." I talked a little too loud at first because I didn't think callers could hear me, but I started talking normally after the trainer reassured me that I could be heard just fine.

About two months passed and I was doing okay; four months passed and I was doing a little better. Then six months passed, I'd done my probation and was on full time. It was difficult at times, but I thought, I can whip this monster. I've always striven to be real good at anything I've ever done.

I stayed there two and a half years. Then my family moved again, and I looked for a new job in the Chapel Hill area.

**What does this job involve?**
We provide all police, fire and EMS communications for the entire county. It runs like a well-oiled machine.

When I came here in '85, I had police dispatch down pretty good, although I had to learn more about fire and especially EMS. I had to learn geographical areas. We have three police departments, the sheriff's department, eight volunteer and two paid fire departments, and four EMS stations.

We're not CAD yet, although we're getting ready to switch over to a computer. Right now we have to write out a complaint card for each call. If I'm call taking, I document all the information and hand it to the communicator who's working that particular department. They read the card and dispatch the call.

We're supposed to have five on a shift, but we're short right now—we have only four or sometimes just three people a shift. We work 12 hours, 7 A.M. to 7 P.M. We also rotate day and night shifts every other week.

**How long was it before you felt confident on the job?**
It was about four years before I could say I'd mastered it really well. The decisions you make may be split-second decisions, and they could mean life, limb or property. In my job, when I sit down, put that headset on and plug in, my stress level is high for 12 hours.

I've had a lot of training since I've been with Orange County. Now I'm an EMD—emergency medical dispatcher. If someone calls and says, "My husband's unconscious and he's not breathing,'' I first get the location and notify the ambulance. Then I ask if the caller feels they can provide CPR. If they say "Yes," I can give them instructions over the phone.

**What do you like most about the work?**
When I can see that I have made a difference in someone's life. I like being able to help somebody who appreciates it, who says, "Thank you." I like the camaraderie between the communicators and all the departments, when people say, "You did a great job today—you were always one step ahead of us, you got us what we needed."

**What do you like least?**
Dealing with people who misuse 911. People will call 911 during a storm and say, "My power's out. What do I do?" You tell them to call the electric company. Or they call to tell you that their dog got loose or to ask where they have to go to vote. About 20 percent of callers ask us for telephone numbers; they think we're 411 (directory information.)

**What advice would you have for someone considering this career?**
If you have a strong stomach and can take a lot of criticism and handle pressure very, very well, you may be just the person for the job. But if you'd panic or freeze when somebody would call you and say that someone is breaking into their house or that they're going to be raped, the job's not for you. If you lose control, you create a problem for yourself as well as for the administration.

**Rod Brown**, 40,
telecommunicator, Volusia County
Sheriff's Department Communications Center,
Daytona Beach, Florida
Years in the job: three

**How did you get into dispatch?**
I saw an ad in the paper. I thought I'd like it and I did. I was self-employed in the landscaping business, which I loved, but this is a better job.

**What kind of training did you have?**
We did the training right here. We had about three weeks of classroom training, about 40 hours a week, and several hours of study time afterward.

**What is your computer-aided dispatch system like?**
It's a very complicated program. It shows you what events or calls need to be taken care of. It tells you what units are available and their status. It gives you geographic information—the caller's address, the cross streets, what zone it's in. With CAD there's no more paperwork at all.

**What services does your department provide?**
We first-hand dispatch for the sheriff's department and all fire services in the entire county. For medical emergencies, we have a unique system of dual response here.

I'll give you an example. I pick up 911 and the caller says, "My husband is having a heart attack." I say, "Just a minute ma'am, are you at . . . ." The address shows up on the screen but I have to confirm it because that's where they're calling from, but that's not necessarily where it (the emergency) is happening. So I confirm where the situation is, then I transfer them to the ambulance service, which has the paramedics on the phone who talk to the caller. Then while they're talking to the paramedics, I put a call in the computer for our fire rescue services to also go to that address.

**What was the hardest part of this job at the start?**
Trying to keep up with the training to do everything you're supposed to do. You've got to realize how fast things happen and how fast you have to react. You have to do certain things for certain calls in a timely manner. During training someone is watching you all the time to make sure you've done it, and then they say, hey, you need to do this or that faster.

**How long was it before you felt competent to deal with whatever was on the other end of that line?**
For me, day one. You're going to know in the first week or two. If you can't do it in that time, you'll never be able to do it.

You cannot be a good dispatcher unless you first know how

to take the call. An example: You pick up 911 and a man says, "I'm going to kill myself. I have the gun, I just want you to know." First, you need to try to talk him down: why are you doing this, what brought you to this? You try to maintain a conversation so he thinks you're totally involved with him. At the same time you're putting the call up there (on the computer screen), punching keys, telling everything you can: "Man with gun threatening suicide." You're still trying to keep him calm, and at the same time you need to notify someone to talk to him on the phone and get him some professional help.

I also do the other end (dispatching). I just got fully trained. Now if I'm the dispatcher, I have several things to do: I have to interpret the information the call taker gives me, condense it, notify the road unit and have them respond to the call. I have to notify our supervisor; possibly a chopper if it warrants it; the medical people; a chaplain, whoever else needs to be notified.

Now here's where the coordination comes in: if the road unit comes on the radio "10-97" (meaning he's on the scene), he's going to want to know, Does this man still have a gun in his hand? Will he step outside? The police officer needs to know so he doesn't get shot. Which means the call taker and the dispatcher, even though they're a room apart, are doing two-way communication on the computer.

**What do you like most about the work?**
I work with a bunch of good people, intelligent people. I don't work with any dummies.

**What do you like least?**
Working holidays and weekends. We work two days on and then two days off. Our shifts are 12 hours long. I usually work 6 P.M.. to 6 A.M. We get two 10-minute breaks before lunch if we can, and then about 40 minutes for lunch. We don't get to leave, we have to be available, but we have a kitchen here and a place to eat.

**What accomplishments are you most proud of so far?**
Some of the things I do during the calls. I can help save a child's life. I don't have a direct involvement, but I do my part of the job. It's an everyday thing. I do my job, I help people, and that's it.

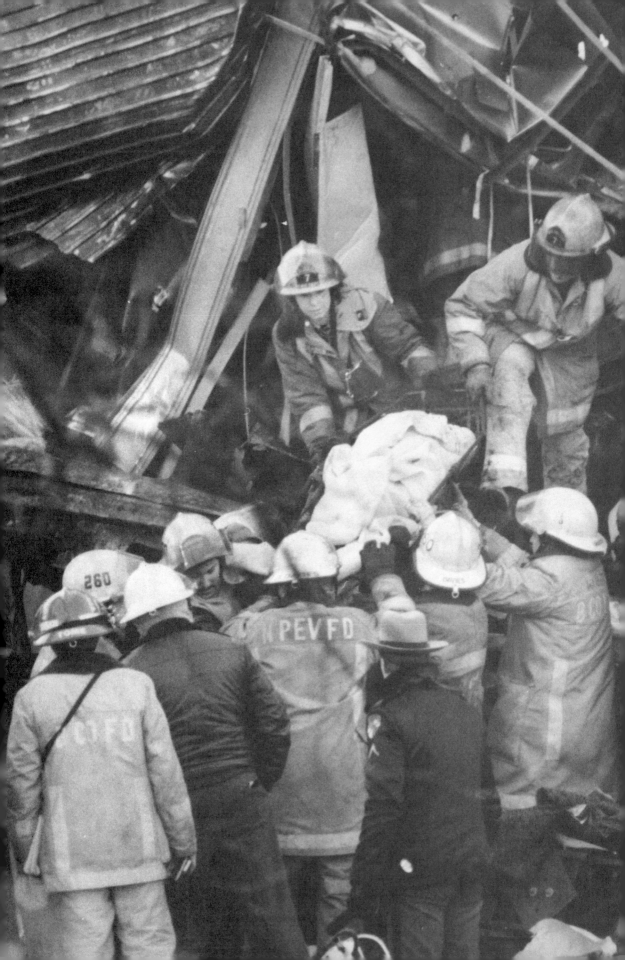

An overturned car dangles precariously down a steep cliff, its injured driver trapped inside. A white water rafter finds the churning waves too much to handle and is flipped into the river. A young skater suddenly plunges through the ice on a rural pond. An inexperienced hiker is lost and frightened as darkness falls upon the mountain. For each of them, the rescuers will come.

Nearly all paid rescue personnel are firefighters, police officers and sheriff's deputies, or emergency medical technicians who have had additional, specialized rescue training. Most typically, they perform their regular law enforcement, ambulance or fire service duties every day and respond to a rescue call as needed. Rescue workers also may be called upon to use their skills after natural disasters such as earthquakes and hurricanes, where hundreds of victims can be trapped in collapsed buildings.

Teams called "Technical Rescue" or "Heavy Rescue" are usually part of urban-area fire departments. Technical rescue involves the use of specialized vehicles, equipment and techniques for such emergencies as building collapses, explosions, train derailments or airplane crashes, vehicle accidents or spills involving toxic chemicals and other hazardous materials. These rescuers are called to find people caught in confined spaces such as storm drains, tunnels or caves, or to free passengers trapped in car wrecks with the use of a powerful hydraulic tool that cuts metal.

Many police or sheriff's departments have a rescue squad or emergency services unit. These officers are specially trained for many emergency medical calls or an event such as "talking down" would-be suicide jumpers. Fire, police or sheriff's departments whose regions include lakes and rivers usually have marine, harbor or dive units with trained public safety divers ready for water-related rescues. River patrol units may use boats specifically designed for rescue operations.

In rural and remote areas, "search and rescue" functions, called SAR, usually fall to sheriff's departments, state police and state or national park rangers. Sheriff's deputies usually manage SAR operations, which generally involve the use of many civilian volunteers, including search dog handlers and experienced cavers. Helicopters are often used, not only when speed is essential, but also in remote or difficult terrain where roads are few or currently impassable due to bad weather.

Wilderness rescue brings special challenges. If a spelunker is trapped in a cave 100 miles from the nearest city, the time it takes rescuers to reach him and transport him to a hospital may be measured in hours or even days, rather than a five-minute ambulance ride. Rescuers may first have to find the victim and then possibly have a strenuous, time-consuming carry-out with him if a helicopter can't fly in or is unavailable. Because the rescuers aren't driving up in an ambulance with all its medical supplies, they often have to improvise with simple, portable equipment, and they must maintain the victim and care for his injuries over a longer period of time. And all of this may have to be done in severe weather such as a snowstorm.

Rescue work is a tall order that not everyone can fill. If it appeals to you, you should also read the chapters in this book on police officers, firefighters and EMTs. You'll need basic training before you can specialize.

## Getting into the Field

### What You Need to Know

(some of the things listed below depend on your rescue specialty)

❑ Vehicle extrication techniques (e.g., how to get victims out of a car wreck)

❑ High-angle rope rescue techniques (e.g., for building walls, cliff faces, cars in ravines)

❑ Wilderness search and rescue techniques

❑ Lake, river and coastal water search techniques

❑ Techniques of diving and equipment use

❑ Ice rescue techniques

❑ Building collapse, trench rescue techniques

❑ Confined space rescue techniques (e.g., manholes, silos, storage bins)

### Necessary Skills

(some of the things listed below depend on your rescue specialty)

❑ Navigation (how to use a map and compass)

❑ Outdoor survival skills

❑ Mechanical aptitude to handle tools and equipment

❑ First aid, CPR (a set of skills that can revive a person who has stopped breathing or whose heart has stopped)

❑ How to swim and/or scuba dive

❑ How to ski and/or snowshoe

❑ Basic rockclimbing

❑ Backpacking, mountaineering

## *Do You Have What It Takes?*

❏ Self-confidence, a "can do" attitude
❏ Ability to improvise and think on your feet
❏ Courage to face dangerous situations
❏ Emotional stability
❏ Ability to react quickly and sensibly under stress
❏ Reliability, strong sense of responsibility (people's lives may depend on you)
❏ Strong desire to serve the public

## *Physical Attributes*

❏ Excellent overall health and physical stamina
❏ Good upper body strength (heavy lifting of victims and/or equipment, sometimes over a considerable distance, is often required)
❏ Good aerobic capacity (necessary for public safety divers, firefighters and other rescue specialists who must use a breathing apparatus to carry out a rescue)
❏ Manual dexterity (e.g., to tie rope knots)

## *Education*

High school diploma generally required

## *Licenses Required*

Driver's license generally required. Rescuers who work primarily as emergency medical technicians (EMTs) must have state certification.

**Competition for jobs:** very competitive

◆ **Job Outlook**

In most areas, there is a great pool of applicants for law enforcement positions or paid jobs as firefighters. Most EMTs are volunteers, but the highest rank, EMT-paramedics, are in greatest demand for paid positions.

Once you are in the police or fire department, generally it is highly competitive to get into the specially trained rescue unit. Experience in construction can be a plus, especially for those interested in technical rescue teams. Though already being a recreational scuba diver can help someone interested in dive rescue, becoming a certified public safety diver requires a great deal of additional training (such as how to do a search pattern, how to retrieve evidence, or how to identify and document a crime scene).

**The Ground Floor**

**Entry-level job:** police officer, firefighter or EMT

**On-the-Job Responsibilities**

*Entry-Level and Experienced Rescue Specialists*

❏ Take specially equipped rescue vehicle, boat or helicopter to rescue site
❏ Locate victim and assess trauma, monitor vital signs
❏ Apply bandages, splints, immobilize fractures, etc.
❏ Provide basic or advanced life support as needed
❏ Secure victim in stretcher or backboard for ''hike out,'' or hoist into helicopter
❏ Swim from boat, dock or shore to rescue site
❏ Assist in the rescue or recovery of drowning victims (many cold-water near drownings may result in a save)

**When You'll Work**

Rescue team members generally work a normal shift, such as a 24-hour tour in a fire department, answering rescue calls on an as-needed basis. If they are off duty, they may be called in if extra assistance is needed or to cover for a rescue specialist who is responding to an emergency. As a result, schedules are often flexible and may be rearranged from day to day.

**Time Off**

Rescue specialists may get extra ''comp'' days off because of the erratic nature of their workweek. Otherwise, they get the normal vacation and holidays that the department gets.

❏ Same job benefits as other employees in police, fire and EMS departments

❏ Free use of facilities during their leisure time (those who work for vacation or ski resorts)

◆ **Perks**

❏ Police or fire department dive rescue squads
❏ Fire department technical/heavy rescue units
❏ County/regional emergency services departments
❏ Federal and state park services
❏ County sheriff's departments
❏ Major vacation and ski resorts

◆ **Who's Hiring**

## *Land-Based Rescue*

◆ **On-the-Job Hazards**

❏ Threat of injury in unstable terrain, be it an urban building collapse or mountain rockslide
❏ In wilderness areas, possibility of extended exposure to adverse weather conditions, which could cause frostbite and hypothermia (condition in which body temperature falls dangerously low) or, in the desert, the possibility of heat stroke and dehydration
❏ In confined spaces, the potential for bad atmospheric conditions (poor oxygen level or toxic substances) may lead to asphyxiation (breathing becomes severely impaired or impossible)
❏ In some desert, rural or mountainous terrain, bites from natural residents such as snakes or insects or exposure to poisonous plants
❏ Risk of helicopter crash during air rescue

## *Water-Related Rescue*

❏ Danger of being swept away by flood waters or river rapids during a swift-water rescue attempt
❏ Pollution, especially in some urban harbors. Water-borne contaminants include chemical pollutants and disease-producing organisms such as bacteria and viruses.

❏ Risk to divers of pressure-related injuries and illnesses such as lung expansion injuries or inner-ear disturbances, including vertigo or infections

## Places You'll Go

**Beginners and experienced rescuers:** occasional travel
Depending on the kind of training you need to get, you may have to travel to an appropriate locale. Fees and out-of-town travel expenses may be paid by the employer.

## Surroundings

The environment changes with each call for help and the region being served. One day you may find yourself at an urban construction site collapse or part of a flash flood that's raging down on a normally dry river bed.

While awaiting the next call, rescuers usually are on duty at their respective home bases—the firehouse, ambulance corps or the police or sheriff's station. Those who work 24-hour shifts generally are provided with sleeping and dining facilities.

## Dollars and Cents

Generally, rescue specialists earn the norm for their grade and longevity in their respective departments. However, some departments may offer a slight upgrade in salary, perhaps one percent, for the completion of a technical training regimen such as confined space rescue or high-angle rope rescue.

## Moving Up

Since rescue work is essentially a sideline to the primary role of the firefighter, EMT or law enforcement officer, the career ladder remains the same. At whatever point rescue team members may decide to leave the "action," they often become instructors in their specialty, either for their department or for a private firm. Others may leave their primary field to go into sales and consulting for the manufacturers of any of the many kinds of specialized rescue equipment.

Paid positions are concentrated in cities and heavily populated regions, which generally have specialized rescue units as part of the municipal police or fire departments. In rural and remote areas, search and rescue is primarily the job of state police or county sheriffs' departments, who oversee the rescue effort conducted almost entirely by volunteers.

Law enforcement, fire and EMS departments usually arrange for employees to get the technical training required for the various rescue specialties. Employees may be sent to a training site for a week or more of intensive coursework, or instructors may be brought in to the home base.

Technical rescue teams generally are part of municipal fire departments and as a result are overwhelmingly male, although increasingly more women are becoming involved with and recruited for fire and rescue services.

### The Bad News

- Unpredictable nature of calls can be stressful
- Erratic shiftwork can be tough on family life
- Threat of injury during a rescue
- Frequent exposure to adverse weather conditions

### The Good News

- Immediate rewards for your efforts
- Never doing the same job twice
- Excitement of being part of the action
- Great responsibility and challenge

Your local police, fire or ambulance squad can tell you whether specially trained professional rescue units serve your area and how current employees get into them.

Organizations for rescue specialists are not a primary source for potential recruits, but they can provide general

**Where the Jobs Are**

**Training**

**The Male/Female Equation**

**Making Your Decision: What to Consider**

**More Information Please**

information about what they offer those already in the field, and about a local chapter or contact.

Dive Rescue Inc., International
201 North Link Lane
Ft. Collins, Colorado 80524-2712
303-482-0887

Dive Rescue trains 10,000 students a year in all aspects of water rescue, predominantly for public safety dive teams. Dive Rescue supports a nonprofit organization for water rescue personnel, the International Association of Dive Rescue Specialists.

National Association for Search and Rescue (NASAR)
P.O. Box 3709
Fairfax, Virginia 22038
703-352-1349

NASAR members include volunteers and professionals involved in all aspects of search and rescue. Among other courses, the nonprofit educational organization offers a wilderness medicine training program for current EMTs and also publishes *Response* magazine quarterly.

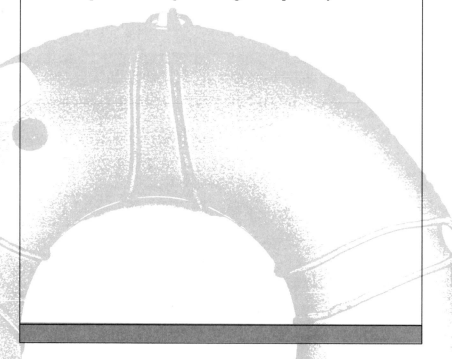

**Tom Price,** 35,
deputy sheriff, Pima County Sheriff's
Department Search and Rescue (SAR),
Tucson, Arizona
Years in the field: 14

**How did you get into rescue work?**
Before joining the department, I was a paramedic with an ambulance squad. I had my associate degree in allied health professions. Getting into law enforcement was a natural progression for me.

I started out on patrol. But after only about eight or nine months I learned that the special weapons team (SWAT) was expanding. They needed a medic on the team, so I went to SWAT. They do high-profile warrant services, a lot of narcotics entries. From there I got into a specialized plainclothes unit.

I was able to maintain my paramedic (certification) and they placed me in a backup role for Search and Rescue (SAR). If the SAR deputies were on vacation or leave I was able to back them up. I did that for a number of years and learned on the job.

91

**How long have you been in SAR?**
Nine years full-time. We have 350 deputies, and two of us do full-time SAR with three backups.

We have flexible duty hours. Generally we go into the office on a dayshift, unless we have something unique planned or there's special training. If I'm the SAR duty officer for the day and any call comes in for a rescue, missing person, that kind of thing, I would be the person notified. The partner on call would be contacted next if we got two SAR incidents at the same time.

If I were called out at midnight, for example, and worked throughout the early morning, I could just flex my time and consider those my duty hours.

**Why does your area require full-time SAR?**
We cover a 9,000-square-mile county, with Tucson and its 700,000 people as the center. There's a lot of rural terrain. Tucson is essentially in a valley of four different mountain ranges. The northern range, the Catalinas, is very accessible; roads go nearly to the wilderness area there. Its accessibility and its closeness to town brings a lot of activity. The area has been written up in climbing guides, and it's not unusual to hear climbers up there speaking Japanese or German. It attracts enthusiasts from all over.

**What do your emergency calls generally involve?**
Our search operations tend to be with people who underestimated the time it was going to take them to do a particular difficult hike, or they underestimated the terrain. Our rescues tend to be orthopedic-type injuries—a broken knee, ankle or leg. We do get our occasional level-one trauma (serious injury) when someone really takes a fall.

We go in on foot for the most part, but we also use horses or call in canines. We have a whole number of different resources we can use.

**What additional training did you have for the job?**
I attended a number of the training sessions that our SAR volunteers had. It helped them to know me and helped me to know what their capabilities were. I've also gone through pretty extensive training for incident management. We have an SAR coordinators association, and we put on an annual

training session. At our last one, we utilized computer assistance programs for search management. Such a program will tell you that you've searched this trail X number of times and you need to be looking elsewhere. There's always something new, new techniques, innovative ways of getting people out.

**Do you have a busy season for rescues?**
During the summer, we'll get torrential rain. At such times people who are used to driving through a dry river bed are suddenly in a flash flood situation, which can be hazardous. They might have driven across that spot earlier when the water was a little trickle; then they come back later and get swept downstream.

**Don't they realize the danger?**
I don't know. They go around barricades, they think they can make it, they want to knock off a few minutes on their drive time, they don't want to be bothered.

If it's a motorist who went around a barricade or is possibly DUI (driving under the influence of drugs or alcohol) and we pull off a rescue, we charge them with endangerment. Not so much because the rescuers were placed in jeopardy, but because they might have endangered others' lives. If they have small children in the vehicle, we'll use that for the charge.

**What do you like most about your work?**
There's nothing routine about it. Even though you may have ten fall victims at the same place, there's always going to be some unique twist. It's still challenging and fun. Being out in the wilderness is an added bonus.

Even the aspect of pulling out someone who's deceased . . . even though you're giving a family notification of a tragic occurrence, it gives them closure, and they realize that.

**What do you like least?**
Though I like the flexibility, sometimes the hours tend to be long and involved. You get called out at all times, and you're not able to plan things. So there's some family time you miss.

**What are you most proud of in your career so far?**
Being able to pull off a technical type of thing and have
people say it was done in a safe manner. Being that we are
a real high-profile type of assignment, we do get that recog-
nition. (Editor's note: Deputy Price took part in a dramatic
helicopter mountain rescue that was later featured on a television show.)

**What advice would you give someone interested in the
work you do?**
I'd recommend it. The whole aspect of law enforcement
and SAR is very positive.

You do have to be physically fit. We still use the standard
physical agility test stuff, plus we incorporate a swim. We
do that every six months just to maintain. We wouldn't be
able to do our job if we weren't physically fit. To coordi-
nate a rescue at a rescue site you have to be able to GET to
the rescue site.

**Keene Black,** 36,
master firefighter, Virginia Beach,
Virginia Fire Department
Technical Rescue Team
Years in the field: 17

**How did you get interested in firefighting and rescue
work?**
I started out as a volunteer firefighter when I was still in
high school. I've also always worked in construction. Be-
yond that, I just like to help people.

In our technical team, we are firefighters day to day, working normal shifts (24 hours on, 48 off). It isn't like we're
only assigned to the technical unit and that's it. We really
have three job functions: we respond to fire calls, EMS
assists (emergency medical services) and technical rescue.
If a technical team call comes in, then we respond with the
appropriate equipment.

**What kind of call brings out the technical team?**
Any call that will tax local resources. What I mean is, 90

percent of the equipment on the technical team are things that you don't see in the average fire department. We have specialized equipment like seismic-type listening devices (for underground rescues), remote control video cameras and breathing apparatus that's not used in normal fire-fighting.

We provide technical rescue service to over a million people in the Tidewater region. We help in disasters, too; we went to Charleston (South Carolina) for Hurricane Hugo in '89.

**When did you get into technical rescue?**
In 1976 I got involved with the heavy squad truck that did vehicle extrication. I'm good with my hands, and I like to do a lot of mechanical and technical type stuff. Years later, I went through all the extra classes.

Heavy-rescue school is all the basic (technical) modules—confined space 1, vehicle 1, rope vertical 1 (high-angle rope rescue) and trench 1. Most trench accidents involve construction sites. (A trench is any cut in the earth deeper than it is wide.)

Now I'm an instructor myself I teach for the state with a team of instructors that goes around Virginia teaching heavy tactical school. Once a year in Virginia Beach we do all the modules at once, a 60-hour class for six days in a row. I've taught people who have come from as far as Australia and Alaska to attend it.

**Who gets on the technical rescue team?**
Each member has been a firefighter for at least two years, is certified as a state level-three firefighter and as an EMT (emergency medical technician), and has been to basic heavy-rescue school.

Firefighters have (training) levels one, two and three. Level-one firefighters can't even go in burning buildings, they can't drive trucks. When they come out of fire school they're level-two firefighters certified by the state, and then within their first year they have to have finished the level-three.

**How many technical rescue calls do you get?**
On average we probably respond to one call a month. This is real specialized stuff.

**What do you like most about your work?**
It's a real big challenge. Most of the calls you get involve people who are really, really in trouble—it's not your every-day false alarm fire call. It involves a lot of hands-on work that not everybody can do. And it's changing every day—there's more technical things coming out all the time. I love doing this stuff.

**What do you like least?**
Seeing all the violence and depression in the everyday world. People getting shot or stabbed, people taking overdoses.

**Who do you think is best suited for this work?**
Somebody good with their hands, who can keep a level head on and think things out on their own. A lot of it is being able to take a situation and figure out how to deal with it—and also being able to recognize when you're getting into a bad situation.

**What advice would you have for someone considering this career?**
In our city it definitely helps to have been a volunteer. Going to fire academy on your own as a volunteer is very helpful. The more training you can get ahead of time, the more likely they'll be to hire you.

But someone coming in should realize that you have to keep up all your training. A lot of people think you get out of the academy and then just ride on the truck. But you can't do that. You've got to stay up on all the technology, stay up on all your training. And once you get all the certifications, you have to keep getting recertified. So you'd better have that commitment.

**Marilyn Kosel,** 30,
technical rescue and dive team,
Tualatin Valley Fire and Rescue/
City of Beaverton Fire Department, Oregon
Years in the field: 12 (six volunteer,
six professional)

**How did you get involved in rescue work?**
I'd always been interested in diving, and when the (technical rescue and dive) team was being formed, I knew I wanted to be on it. I already knew how to swim, so I just needed to get my dive certification. I earned my general "Open Water 1" certificate after about eight weeks of training. Then when I got on the team, they gave us more specialized training in rescue diving techniques and swiftwater rescue.

Getting on the team was hard; it was really competitive. Past experience and ability were very important, and a lot of the guys already had their dive certification. Because I didn't, I was at a disadvantage. I called the captain of the dive team almost on a shift-to-shift basis trying to convince him how badly I wanted to be on the team. Finally I was chosen. I've been on the team for two and a half years now.

**What was hardest at first about learning to dive?**
The hardest thing to get used to was breathing out of a tank. You have to concentrate and stay calm. I had some apprehension at first. Especially as a new diver you don't know what you're going to see down there. Luckily they started us out in a swimming pool—you could see everything clearly and you knew it wasn't that far to the surface.

Then we went to our training pond at the training center, which is a little deeper and darker and full of algae. They have it set up with props in it: a sunken car, a plane; they even have a bus in there. It was so strange the first time I came upon the car while practicing a search pattern. It was covered with green slime, and I could barely recognize it.

**Do you do technical rescue as well?**
Yes. I'm trained to be a high-angle (rope rescue) instructor, and I've been trained through all the heavy rescue—

97

building collapse, confined space, trench rescue. I'm also an EMT (emergency medical technician).

On the combined technical rescue team—the dive, heavy and high angle—there are 33 people, with 15 on the dive team. When we first started, we were all in one station, and we were all trained in everything. Then about a year ago they split the dive team away.

**Is firefighting your primary duty unless there's a dive call?**
Yes. At our station we have a (pumper) engine, advanced life support rescue vehicle, and what we call the squad (the dive van) and the boat. If we get a dive call we take all the apparatus. We have neoprene dry suits we wear on most calls and training exercises and also a dry suit made from a latex-type material that we use for contaminated water because it's better sealed. We're mainly concerned about farming ponds; they can be full of all kinds of chemicals.

We've been on several rescues or recoveries (finding a drowning victim). We also do work for the sheriff's department such as looking for evidence—we searched for a gun in one of the rivers here. Off duty, we'll search for people's stuff if they've dropped something out of a boat or off the dock.

**What do you like most about your job?**
Every day when I go to work we do something different. It's not monotonous, and it's always challenging.

**What do you like least?**
Well, I hope I never have to recover a body. I've been part of a recovery search team, but luckily I've never been the one who actually finds the body. I admit I'm not looking forward to that.

**What are you most proud of so far in your career?**
I'm just proud to have the job. I was hired in '86, and I was the first and only woman in the department for five years. Today, there are five women out of 270 uniformed firefighters.

Unfortunately, when I was hired, before I even came on, everyone was really uptight about having a woman on the job. But I was so unaware of it at the time that I just always acted like myself; I wasn't trying to prove anything. The guys would ask me: "What are you trying to prove? Why are you here?" I'd say I'm not trying to prove anything; I just want this job for the same reasons you do—I like the hours, the pay's good and it's challenging.

**Do you feel accepted now?**
I believe I'm accepted by the guys who know me well, the guys I actually work with. That's not a problem. But there are still a lot of stereotypes out there. It's the people who don't know me who have all these opinions.

There was one nice thing—when they split up the technical teams both sides wanted me. That was kind of neat. The heavy/high angle team members wanted me to come to their station; I had more training than a lot of them had. And the dive section also called and said, "Marilyn, we'd really like to have you come." I was actually pretty proud of that.

**When you first applied to the fire department, did you have the difficulty most women do with the physical entry tests?**
I never stopped to think whether I could do it—I just did it, and luckily I was strong enough. I'm 5 feet 4 inches, and I weighed about 150 pounds at the time. My background helped; I was raised mostly on a farm. I didn't have any brothers, so my three sisters and I did all the work. I went through my childhood just believing I could do things. And if I couldn't do something, I'd figure out a way to do it through mechanical advantage or leverage. I was familiar with power tools, and I really think that gave me a great advantage.

Most women do tend to have more problems with upper body strength, but a lot of that can be overcome with learned technique, along with strength training. That's why it's really important to practice those skills before you go in to take the test. I tell people all the time: "Call me up and I'll take you to our training center." I take them through the components of the test and let them practice the techniques. A lot of firefighters are willing to help people who want to learn.

# WILL YOU FIT INTO THE WORLD OF EMERGENCY AND PROTECTIVE SERVICES?

*If you can picture yourself in a police uniform, patrolling a beat as one of society's protectors, take this quiz:*

Read each statement, then rate how you feel about it by choosing number 0, 5 or 10 according to the following scale:

**0** = Disagree
**5** = Agree somewhat
**10** = Strongly agree

\_\_\_I'm a disciplined and highly motivated person

\_\_\_I find it easy to communicate with people, from children to the elderly

\_\_\_I can remain calm in an emergency and decide what to do next

\_\_\_I can be patient and tolerant even when others are being difficult

\_\_\_I'm service oriented and want to contribute something to my community

\_\_\_I understand that there are all kinds of people and two sides to every story

\_\_\_I think I could handle weapons and face dangerous people and situations

\_\_\_I like the idea that every day has a routine, yet each one can be unpredictable

\_\_\_I think that I have a lot of common sense

\_\_\_I like the idea of working outdoors a lot of the time

Now add up your score.    ___Total points

If your total points were less than 50, you probably don't have sufficient interest in policing, or the inclination to learn what's required. If your total points were between 50 and 75, you may have what it takes to get into the field, but be sure to do more investigation by following the suggestions at the beginning of this section. If your total points were 75 or more, it's highly likely that you are a good candidate for a career as a cop.

***If the sound of the neighborhood firehouse alarm makes you wish you could be part of the action, take the following quiz:***

Read each statement, then rate how you feel about it by choosing number 0, 5 or 10 according to the following scale:

**0** = Disagree
**5** = Agree somewhat
**10** = Strongly agree

___I am physically strong, agile and in excellent health

___I can think and act quickly in an emergency

___I'm the dependable type; people know they can count on me

___I'm good with my hands and enjoy physical labor and activities

___I believe I could help someone else, even at the potential risk of my own safety

___I usually get along well with others and am even tempered

___I can concentrate on getting a task done amid "organized chaos"

___I believe I have a lot of common sense and can figure out what a situation requires

___I like to see immediate results for my efforts

___I like being part of a team, working toward a common goal

Now add up your score.    ___Total points

If your total points were less than 50, you probably do not have sufficient interest in the fire service, or the inclination to learn what's required. If your total points were between 50 and 75, you may have what it takes to get into the field, but be sure to do more investigation first by following the suggestions at the beginning of this section. If your total points were 75 or more, it's highly likely that you are a good candidate for a career at the firehouse.

*If you think you'd like to be an emergency medical technician, ready to give care at a moment's notice, take this quiz:*

Read each statement, then rate how you feel about it by choosing number 0, 5 or 10 according to the following scale:

> **0** = Disagree
> **5** = Agree somewhat
> **10** = Strongly agree

___I have compassion for the suffering of others and want to help them

___I am a good observer and pay attention to detail

___I'm not squeamish about blood or seeing someone's injuries

___I can perform well under pressure

___I am healthy and in good physical shape, with no back problems

___I am interested in learning a lot about the human body—biology, anatomy, physiology, etc.

___I have the patience to deal with people who are upset, in pain or even unappreciative of my efforts

___I believe I could handle being responsible for someone else's life

___I can communicate easily with people I've just met

___I am willing to keep up with the latest techniques (through classroom study and formal training)

Now add up your score.     ___Total points

If your total points were less than 50, you probably do not have sufficient interest in becoming an EMT or the inclination to learn what's required. If your total points were between 50 and 75, you may have what it takes to get into the field, but be sure to do more investigation first by following the suggestions at the beginning of this section. If your total points were 75 or more, it's highly likely that you are a good candidate for a seat on the ambulance.

### *If you like the idea of helping dozens of people a day by dispatching the services they need, take the following quiz:*

Read each statement, then rate how you feel about it by choosing number 0, 5 or 10 according to the following scale:

> **0** = Disagree
> **5** = Agree somewhat
> **10** = Strongly agree

\_\_\_\_I am a good listener

\_\_\_\_I can get information that I need by asking the right questions

\_\_\_\_I stay calm under pressure and have a "strong stomach"

\_\_\_\_I speak well and can clearly convey instructions and information

\_\_\_\_It doesn't fluster me to do more than one thing at a time

\_\_\_\_I have the patience to handle difficult people

\_\_\_\_I can write information down without making a mistake

\_\_\_\_I enjoy working with computers and specialized equipment

\_\_\_\_I wouldn't mind working in one place all day

\_\_\_\_I have good concentration

\_\_\_\_I'm not a nervous or restless type of person

Now add up your score. \_\_\_\_Total points

If your total points were less than 50, you probably do not have sufficient interest in becoming an emergency dispatcher or the inclination to learn what's required. If your total points were between 50 and 75, you may have what it takes to get into the field, but be sure to do more investigation by following the suggestions at the beginning of this section. If your total points were 75 or more, it's highly likely that you are a good candidate for this career.

### *If being a member of a highly trained, ready-for-anything rescue team holds great appeal for you, take this quiz:*

Read each statement, then rate how you feel about it by choosing number 0, 5 or 10 according to the following scale:

**0** = Disagree
**5** = Agree somewhat
**10** = Strongly agree

\_\_\_I believe I can handle most any situation
\_\_\_I like the idea of helping people who are in trouble
\_\_\_I like the challenge of identifying a problem and figuring out its solution
\_\_\_I can improvise when necessary and think on my feet
\_\_\_I enjoy working as part of a team
\_\_\_I'm not easily upset and can roll with the punches
\_\_\_I'm adept with tools and equipment and don't mind getting my hands dirty
\_\_\_I'm the physical type; I have a great deal of stamina and strength, and I like to stay in shape
\_\_\_I have a lot of determination and don't give up easily
\_\_\_I believe I am courageous and could face a dangerous situation sensibly without taking foolish risks

Now add up your score.    \_\_\_Total points

If your total points were less than 50, you probably do not have sufficient interest in becoming a rescue worker or the inclination to learn what's required. If your total points were between 50 and 75, you may have what it takes to get into the field, but be sure to do more investigation first by following the suggestions at the beginning of this section. If your total points were 75 or more, it's highly likely that you are a good candidate for this career.